D1528808

A Storyteller's Guide
To Joyful Service

Turning Your
Misery into Ministry

Tony Agnesi

Virtu Press

Wadsworth, Ohio

© 2012–2018 Tony Agnesi

All rights reserved. No part of this book may be reproduced by any means in any form, photocopied, recorded, electronic or otherwise, without the written permission from the author except for brief quotations in a review.

Scripture texts in this work are taken from the *New American Bible, revised edition* © 2010, 1991, 1986, 1970 Confraternity of Christian Doctrine, Washington, D.C. and are used by permission of the copyright owner. All Rights Reserved. No part of the New American Bible may be reproduced in any form without permission in writing from the copyright owner.

Printed in the United States of America

ISBN-13: 978-0692147245 (Virtu Press)

ISBN-10:0692147241

The author is donating 100 percent of the net proceeds from this book to the charities and ministries he and his wife support. Many of these charities and ministries are mentioned in his books.

Dedication

To my wife, Diane:

Of all the gifts and blessings that God has granted me, none comes close to the blessings I received having you in my life. I am so thankful that we fell in love at such a young age and that our love is still growing stronger every day in our Christ-centered marriage. We've been through a lot together—good times, scary times, hard times, and wonderful times. Through it all, you have never wavered in your love for me, or your dedication to God, your family, and friends. You are the love of my life.

Always and forever,

Tony

Michael & Marli

Blessings!

Tony

Table of Contents

Chapter 3- God's Grace in Hard Times

Chapter 4 — God's Grace in the Virtues

Introduction

Hard times; everyone has them. During the course of our lives, we will suffer the pain of the loss of loved ones. We will have medical issues, job losses, and/or marital problems. Others will become addicted to alcohol, drugs, sex, pornography, and/or shopping. God never promised us a pain-free, problem-free life. He did promise us the grace to get through it all.

In *A Storyteller's Guide to a Grace-Filled Life*, I shared stories of the grace that comes through our families, living the virtues, sharing the holidays, our day-to-day lives, and through our prayer life.

This book is different. In *A Storyteller's Guide to Joyful Service*, I'll share stories of hard times, both my own and others. In each, I will try to show the ways that God's grace helped to navigate a way through the pain, suffering, guilt, and shame. Ultimately, I show how many people take these difficult times and turn them into a lifetime apostolate. They turn their misery into a ministry.

From hard times to taking action, these stories will highlight putting that action into service. This is a service that only comes from having been there and done that. I'll show you people that have turned their suffering into a mission and have not only changed their lives but the lives of the people around them through God's amazing grace.

Each story is framed in scripture and following each story are a few questions for reflection. These questions are written to help you put yourself in the story and find your own truth.

Like *A Storyteller's Guide to a Grace-Filled Life*, these stories can be read all at once, or one at a time. Many readers of my first book have remarked that they have it on their nightstand and read one or two stories before bedtime, allowing the message to resonate in their subconscious as they sleep. Others have used the stories in the morning, along with their morning prayers, offerings, and Bible readings. Still others have shared the stories with prayer groups, book clubs, and/or Bible studies. They use the stories and reflections as conversation starters for group discussion.

May each of these stories bless you and help you to recall the stories that have molded your life in Christ. May they help you turn your misery into ministry. That is my prayer, my friend.

CHAPTER ONE

God s Grace in Service

Lord, Make Me an Instrument

> But you will receive power when
> the Holy Spirit comes upon you,
> and you will be my witnesses in Je-
> rusalem, throughout Judea and
> Samaria, and to the ends of the
> earth. (Acts 1:8, NAB)

Lord, make me an instrument; put someone in front of me today
that you can help through me.

I pray this little prayer every morning as I receive the Blessed Sac-
rament at Mass. I've been doing it for several years now. It is a
powerful prayer, and if you are sincere, it works every time. For
me, it is the single most powerful way that God shows his presence as he uses me to do his work.

I began doing this after reading two books that had an impact on
the way I looked at serving the Lord. One was, *Ten Prayers God Al-*

ways Says Yes To, by Anthony DeStefano[1] and the other was, *You Were Born for This* by Bruce Wilkinson.[2]

Anthony said this prayer is "so potent that if it were sold in a supermarket, it would have to come with a warning label: Don't pray this unless you are prepared for instant results!"[3] If this sounds like an exaggeration, it is NOT! It works 100 percent of the time and it works every day. Not a day goes by that I don't experience God putting someone in my day that I can help. I just need to be open, keep listening, and the get out of the way long enough for the Holy Spirit to do his thing.

God has been using people as instruments since creation, and you can participate by simply checking in for duty. Bruce says it just takes a small shift in how we think. Tomorrow morning why not join me. Say this little prayer and check in for duty. Then watch what happens!

Reflection: *Do you "check in for duty" each day and ask God to put someone in your path that you can help? When people ask for your prayers, do you ever drop everything and pray for them right then?*

She Called Me an Angel

> Let mutual love continue. Do not
> neglect hospitality, for through it
> some have unknowingly entertained
> angels. (Hebrews 13:1–2, NAB)

Glancing at my busy schedule today, I noticed that I have a strategic planning session coming up for the Community Pregnancy Center of Barberton, Ohio. Several times each year, I get to meet with the board and plan their strategy for running this very worthwhile ministry. I couldn't help but remember my first experience with CPC.

It was almost 20 years ago when I read in the church bulletin that the Community Pregnancy Center was in need of infant formula. I inquired around and learned that the Center helps new mothers who can't afford formula. Through this program, new mothers are given enough to meet their needs until they get help from WIC or some other program.

Thinking that this was a worthwhile endeavor, I made my way on Saturday morning to the local grocery store to buy formula. It had been a long time since I bought any formula, and I was surprised at how much it had gone up in price. "Wow!" I thought. "I wonder how any young couple could afford this."

I decided to purchase five cases of formula using a check I received for a speaking engagement earlier that week. Looking at the shelf, I remembered the name *Similac* from my past. I leaned over and loaded cases on the cart. They only had four. I asked the stock clerk if there were any more in the back, and after looking, he said no, the four cases were all they had. Glancing back at the shelf, I saw another product called *Enfamil*. Reading the can, I learned that it was for babies who couldn't digest regular formula. I don't know why, but something told me to buy it, so I threw a case of *Enfamil* in the cart and went to the checkout.

Arriving at the Community Pregnancy Center, located in a small house on the main drag, I walked up to the back door and was greeted by an elderly volunteer. I told her I was delivering some formula. She held the door for me as I carried two cases at a time into the tiny kitchen. Then it was back to the car for the case of *Enfamil*.

As I entered the kitchen, Pat Shea, the director of the center, introduced herself and said, "Is that *Enfamil* you are carrying?"

"Yes," I replied. "They ran out of *Similac*, so I was forced to buy a case of Enfamil."

"Well," she exclaimed, "the Holy Spirit must be working overtime today! You see, we have a client in my office right now whose baby can only digest *Enfamil*. I was just telling her that we were out of it and couldn't help her baby! Would you mind carrying it out to her car?"

As I was walking out of the house, Pat returned to her office and I overheard her say to the young girl, "It's a miracle, an ANGEL just dropped off the formula you need!"

"An angel," I thought. The young girl thanked me. The volunteer thanked me, and Pat thanked me as I said, "I'll be back again!"

Coincidence? I don't think so. I did return many times. I still do today with formula, diapers, and baby clothes.

As I look back over my life, I've been called lots of things, mostly negative, but there is something about the sound of the word *Angel* that makes me smile.

Reflections: *Have you ever done something for someone that just happened to be the right thing at the right time? Do you feel that these occurrences are just coincidence? Have you ever felt you received more than you gave when this happened?*

Serving with Compassion

Put on then, as God's chosen ones, holy and beloved, heartfelt compassion, kindness, humility, gentleness, and patience. (Colossians 3:12 NAB)

When we hear of someone who is suffering, we feel sorry for them; we have feelings of pity and empathy. If someone loses a loved one, a job, or has an incurable illness or accident, we feel these emotions.

Are these emotions compassion or something else?

Compassion is literally defined as to suffer together. It is often described as the heart that trembles in the face of suffering. We are compassionate when we take on that suffering and are moved to relieve it. Compassionate people can feel what others are feeling. It may be because they know what it is like to suffer. Compassionate people act with kindness.

> [And] be kind to one another,
> compassionate, forgiving one an-
> other as God has forgiven you in
> Christ. (Ephesians 4:32 NAB)

Compassionate people practice self-compassion as well. By being compassionate to ourselves, we will be more successful in changing a bad habit, getting back to the gym, or eating a healthier diet. There are many health benefits from being a more compassionate person. Studies have shown compassion creates an increase in the hormones that counter aging and reduce stress.

What are some of the ways you can practice being a more compassionate person? How can increasing our compassion better help us serve others?

Here are a few ideas:

- Act on your feelings of empathy and pity. When you hear of someone suffering, have the courage to act on it. Try sending them a card or make a phone call and encourage them.
- Practice random acts of kindness. Simple gestures like smiling, saying hello, and thank you are a start. Inviting someone to lunch, or spending some one-on-one time with a suffering friend, can work wonders.
- Be kind. As the old saying goes, "Be kind, because everyone you meet is fighting a battle you know nothing about." By showing compassion, you will help them open up and share what is on their hearts.

- Be grateful. Being grateful for our blessings helps us to better serve those going through hard times. We all will experience tough times in our lives and our ability to cope is increased by our compassion for others.
- Sometimes a hug will speak louder than anything you can say. Without a word, it says I'm here for you; I feel your pain and will do what I can to help.

As we seek to serve others as our Lord asks, let's practice being compassionate people. Let's act on our feelings of empathy. It will be a blessing to the people we meet and it will have many health benefits, as well. Who can argue with that?

Reflections: *What might you do to be a more compassionate person? What do you think of the concept of suffering together? Do you practice self-compassion?*

The Homeless Bible Study

God is faithful and will not let you be tried beyond your strength; but with the trial he will also provide a way out, so that you may be able to bear it. (1 Corinthians 10:13, NAB)

Every Friday night, the folks at Springtime of Hope help feed and clothe the needy in and around St. Bernard's Church in downtown Akron. A wonderful Friday night meal is served along with the distribution of shoes, blankets, tarps, coats, and gloves.

As the season of Advent began, my friend Jeff asked if I would facilitate a Bible Study for the homeless on Friday nights, after dinner.

"Who would go to a Bible study during the cold winter months?" I asked.

"I really don't know," he replied, "but we could set it up, announce it at dinner, and see what happens." So, we did.

The first night we had two men stay for the Bible study. I was surprised that they both were carrying Bibles that were well worn from use. Each Friday, the numbers grew—eight, then ten, then fourteen, and the Friday before Christmas day, twenty-five people came. Men and women, young and old, black and white, together we shared.

What resonated with me was the hope each person heard that the Lord would see them through their difficult times. Many were sleeping in tents, in the woods, or in the corner of a parking deck, or in their car; but all had the hope that the Lord would see them through.

This was very humbling for me, knowing that I would return from the cold winter night to a warm house, a comfortable bed, and a hot meal. It reminded me of the verse in 1 Corinthians 10:13 about God's faithfulness.

As I began to read it aloud from my Bible, nearly half the room recited it with me, word for word, from memory! On the streets, this is the mantra of the homeless.

We discussed God's faithfulness; that we will not be tried beyond our strength, and that the Lord will provide a way out.

That night, something wonderful happened at our little homeless Bible study. We knew that the Holy Spirit was with us. As we were about to conclude, one of the men, a large, imposing man who had spent most of his life in prison, asked if he could sing.

"Sure!" was the reply from the group.

Then, Big Mo with the voice of a trained opera singer, tattered clothes, dirty, disheveled look, clinging to his Bible with chapped hands, sang the most beautiful version of *The Impossible Dream* that I ever heard. A modern day, homeless Don Quixote, believed with all his heart, that God is faithful and won't try us beyond our strength. He will give us a way out of troubles that might seem impossible.

Now, whenever I begin to think that my trials are too much to bear, I think of Big Mo and remember fondly the lessons from that Homeless Bible Study.

Reflections: *Do you ever feel stuck in your current situation without a way out? Do you trust that God will not test you beyond your strength? Do you agree that God is faithful?*

Homeless in Nashville

Then the righteous will answer him and say, "Lord, when did we see you hungry and feed you, or thirsty and give you drink? When did we see you a stranger and welcome you, or naked and clothe you? When did we see you ill or in prison, and visit you?" And the king will say to them in reply, "Amen, I say to you, whatever you did for one of these least brothers of mine, you did for me." (Matthew 25:37–40, NAB)

The people in the parks, the alcoholics, the homeless, they are looking at you. Do not be those who look and

do not see.[4] — Blessed Saint Mother
Teresa of Calcutta

I recently returned from a business trip to Nashville. It was a great time spent with friends, many of which, I get to see just once a year.

The first morning in town, I left the hotel. Not willing to pay $13.95 a day for internet access, I walked a short couple of blocks to the Panera for free Wi-Fi.

As I left the hotel, I made eye contact with the only person walking on the sidewalk at that early hour. From her clothes and disheveled look, I could tell she was homeless. The second I noticed her, I quickly turned my head, looked away, and made my way quickly down the sidewalk.

"Excuse me, sir; excuse me," she said in a loud voice, as I kept on walking. "Excuse me, sir," she said again. As she repeated it for the third time, she was standing right next to me. Grudgingly, I acknowledged her.

"Can you tell me what time it is?" She asked.

"7:30," I replied.

"Thank You," she said, and then she began her story. "I'm from Bristol, you know, near the race track. I've been in Nashville for over a year. There is no work here."

It was a familiar story. Working with the homeless, I've heard it many times. The story is always followed by a request for money. It seemed rehearsed, but when your only means of eating is begging for money, you practice your pitch.

I asked her a few questions as we briskly walked, "Do you know where the nearest shelter is?" "Have you had anything to eat?" I've asked these questions many times to the homeless folks I encountered over the years, but frankly, this time, I wasn't interested in the answers.

By then, I had made it to my destination, and as I did, I turned, handed her a twenty-dollar bill and walked away.

It only took a minute to realize what just happened. During our walk, I made no eye contact with her. I was distant, judgmental, and aloof. Sure, I gave her money, but the thing she needed most - my attention, I denied her.

I remember Mother Theresa (my personal hero) used to "see the face of Jesus" in every homeless person she met. "Minister to the Jesus in front of you," she would say.

The money might help this woman with her next meal, but my time and attention would have been a greater gift. I missed a chance to look into the face of our Lord.

Lord, help me to see your face in everyone I meet.

Reflection: *Have you ever crossed the street to avoid a homeless person? Does Mother Teresa inspire you to approach the homeless in a different way?*

The Homeless Hike

And the crowds asked him, "What then should we do?" He said to them in reply, "Whoever has two cloaks should share with the person who has none. And whoever has food should do likewise." (Luke 3:10–11, NAB)

A few weeks ago, my friend Sean, whom I met through Project Homeless Connect, called me and asked if I would like to go with a small group on a Homeless Hike. Once a month, his group treks along five miles of railroad track where many homeless people set up campsites. The group backpacks the route with bags of food, water, and supplies like toilet paper and tooth paste.

I agreed, and we met the group early one evening. Most were in their late 20's or early 30's. I was the oldest in the group; I realized that my backpacking days ended close to forty years earlier. I was impressed with the group: a female doctor, a young male second year resident, a few social service workers who work with the homeless every day, along with a former co-worker Tina, Sean, and me.

As we walked though woods, weeds, and briars, up and down banks to get to these sites, I reflected on the cause of homelessness.

Drugs, alcohol, mental illness, unemployment, broken homes, domestic violence are the causes. Homelessness is the effect of these problems. We can't cure homelessness unless we deal with these real issues.

One person we visited that night has a skin disease. After the doctor examined him, she was able to schedule him for needed treatment at the hospital the next day.

"Have you seen a doctor about your skin problem?" I heard her ask.

"Yes," he replied, "but I was with the doctor two minutes and he sent me a bill for $300! I can't afford $300."

The young doctor assured him that she had become a doctor to help people and she wouldn't send him a bill. It took her several minutes of convincing him before he finally trusted her.

We visited many campsites that night, some abandoned, some in use with no one there, and still others that were the temporary home for some, at least until the police or the railroad ran them off the property.

Near the end of our hike, we walked along a pair of railroad tracks heading back to our parked cars. Walking toward us, on the same track, was a young man walking his bicycle. When he spotted us, he switched over to the other track, as if he was scared we might be with the railroad.

As he neared us, he stopped for a moment and then yelled over, "Hi Tony!" as he made his way closer to our group. As he got closer, I recognized him as a young man I met three years earlier at a downtown shelter, a place where the homeless can get a Friday night meal.

"Hey Tom, do you need any food or water?" I asked.

"No, I'm good," was his reply.

"Are you sure? This pack is getting heavy on my back, and I'd appreciate lightening the load," I returned in a joking manner.

He paused for a moment, and then said, "There *is* someone else who could use your help further down the tracks. His site is really hidden, but I can take you to him."

"Sure," I replied. "Let's go."

As we made our way through the weeds and brush, we came upon his campsite. "Hey, Mike. Come on out. These are my friends; you can trust them." Tom pointed to the group. We talked with Mike, the doctors examined him, and we left him some food and water.

"Is there anyone else nearby we can help?" I asked Tom.

"Yes, there is a woman, and her dog, living just over the hill, but she's not here now."

"If I give you some food and water, will you deliver it to her?" I asked.

"I sure will, and Tony, I promise that she will get everything you give. I won't take anything for myself."

"I know you will, Tom, because I trust you," I said quietly.

"Why do you trust me, when most people don't?" Tom asked.

"Because three years ago, when I met you at the shelter, I asked you if you needed anything and you said you only needed a roll of toilet paper. I gave you two. Quietly, you gave one of the rolls back and said give it to someone else who needed it. Your selfless-ness made an impression on me, Tom, and I am proud to be your friend."

He smiled a friendly smile and waved as we made our way further down the railroad tracks as the sun began to set.

It's funny about trust. When the man with the skin disease realized that the doctor was not there to make money but to help him, he allowed her to examine him and was very grateful she did. And because of Tom's unselfish gesture three years earlier with a roll of toilet paper, I trusted him.

I guess it is true; no one cares how much you know, until they know how much you care.

Reflections: How does the subject of trust sway your opinion or cause you to pause when dealing with someone you don't know? Do we judge people by their circumstances? How can we be more open to trusting others? Can others trust us?

Debbie, the Good Samaritan

But because he wished to justify himself, he said to Jesus, "And who is my neighbor?" Jesus replied, "A man fell victim to robbers as he went down from Jerusalem to Jericho. They stripped and beat him and went off leaving him half-dead. A priest happened to be going down that road, but when he saw him, he passed by on the opposite side. Likewise, a Levite came to the place, and when he saw him, he passed by on the opposite side. But a Samaritan traveler who came upon him was moved with compassion at the sight. He approached the victim, poured oil and wine over his wounds and bandaged them. Then he lifted him up on his own animal, took him to an inn and cared for him. The next day he took out two silver coins and gave them to the innkeeper with the instruction, 'Take care of him. If you spend more than what I have given you, I shall repay you on my way back.' Which of these three, in your opinion, was neighbor to the robbers' victim?" He answered, "The one who treated him with mercy." Jesus said to him, "Go and do likewise." (Luke 10:29–37)

It had been a long day when I left the Project Homeless Connect event at the Civic Center. Over 450 homeless people received help that day. I felt gratified that I did something to help.

As I walked to my car, parked several blocks away from the event, I noticed a disheveled man leaning against a trash container. I could tell at a glance that he had been on the street a while, but I didn't recognize him from the event. As I walked, I noticed several people crossing the street to avoid him.

On the other side of the street, there appeared to be a lost dog, and many of the people that had avoided the homeless man were gathering around the found puppy.

I thought of the parable of the Good Samaritan in Luke's gospel. Both the priest and the Levite crossed the road to avoid the traveler that had been beaten and left for death.

As I walked toward the man, a young, neatly dressed woman approached him and asked if he needed help. By then, I was near enough to ask if he had been to Project Homeless Connect.

He said, "No." He was unaware the event happened just a couple of blocks away. Aware there was food left over from the event, the young woman and I walked him to the Civic Center. We got him something to eat and introduced him to a shelter director who volunteered to help him find a place to sleep.

As I walked away, I turned to the woman and said, "Thank you for caring." I could tell by the look in her eyes as she fought back tears, that this was a loving, caring person. She was a modern day Good Samaritan.

As I drove home, a report on the radio caught my attention. The newscaster said, "The pet business has become an eight billion dollar industry."

Pet spas, pet parks, pet designer clothing, and gourmet dog food have become commonplace.

"Eight billion dollars," I thought. And this man can't find a meal, shelter, or even get noticed by the people who walked past him to come to the aid of a lost dog!

Project Homeless Connect was cancelled this year for lack of funding. Meanwhile, I bet the pet industry has probably grown by another billion dollars. It is sad, because now while Fido is getting a massage at the doggie spa, the homeless must rely on Good Samaritans like Debbie for their survival.

Reflection: *Have you ever crossed the street to avoid a homeless person? How did it make you feel? Have you ever found yourself in the role of Good Samaritan? How did it make you feel?*

Hey, You Are in My Seat

It was just another winter day as I made my way to St. Bernard's for the 12:10p.m. Mass. St. Bernard's is a beautiful, large church in the middle of downtown. During the week it caters to downtown workers, as well as students from the nearby University of Akron.

I don't know about you, but when I go to daily Mass, I have my own seat. You might have your regular seat too. It's always there, the same seat in the same row on the same side of the church. It's kind of a comfort to know that I have my seat. But not today!

As I walked into Mass, I noticed someone in my seat! This church must have a thousand seats, so why did this person sit in *mine*? Walking down the aisle, I could see a young woman with a book bag, sitting in my seat! I was certain this was a probably a student praying for a good grade on a test for which she didn't study. As I entered the pew, I noticed that the woman was older, perhaps in her early 30's. A little disgusted, I settled in my new seat at the far end of the row as Mass began.

Immediately, I noticed that she seemed new to this church thing. She didn't have a songbook as we began the opening hymn. So, being a good Christian, I handed her mine. She smiled a thank you and moved closer to me in the pew so that we could both see and share the hymnal. As she did, I realized that this wasn't a college student, but a young homeless woman.

As Mass ended, we again shared the hymnal, and as I moved from the pew to leave, she stopped me and asked, "Can I tell you something?"

"OK," I replied.

"I'm homeless and I have an appointment at the courthouse. I must pay a fine of $28, but I was only able to get the money for bus fare downtown. I walked here from the bus station. Since I had time before my appointment with the court, I thought I would come into this church to pray for a miracle."

"Do you see that grey-haired woman in the first pew? She saw me crying and came over to me and asked if she could help. I told her my situation and she took out her checkbook and wrote a check to the court for $28. She told me when the court sees her name on the check that they will accept it." She flashed the check proudly for me to see her miracle, and I couldn't help but notice that the elderly woman's name started with *Judge!* I told her I was excited that she got her miracle and after a God bless you, and have a great day, she stopped me again.

"Sir," she said. "I am hungry and haven't eaten in almost three days."

Normally, I would have given her money for lunch, but this happened to be one of those days when I didn't have any cash with me.

I said, "Walk with me. The University has a café down one block and I'll see if they have an ATM or take credit cards, and I'll get you something to eat."

As we opened the door to the café, I noticed an ATM and it was my bank. I quickly went to the machine and got her enough cash for the day. As I went back to the doorway where she was standing, I noticed that she had only five minutes before her appointment.

I gave her the money and quickly walked her back up the hill to the courthouse. As we walked, I could tell that she was crying. When we reached the courthouse, she gave me the biggest hug and thanked me between the tears.

She sobbed, "I walked into a church for the *first* time today to pray for a miracle, and I got two! God is *so* great!"

Walking away, I couldn't help but think that God had put her into *my* seat so that we could share Mass and a couple of miracles. I've seen her several times at Mass since, and every time she smiles at me and says, "God is *so* great!"

You know, come to think of it, God REALLY IS GREAT!

Reflection: Do you get so set in your ways that you miss opportunities to see God's miracles? Do you ever feel that God is responsible for your encounters? Do you keep yourself open to these nudges from God? Have you ever needed a miracle?

You Give Love a Bad Name

And lying at his door was a poor
man named Lazarus, covered with
sores, who would gladly have eaten
his fill of the scraps that fell from
the rich man's table. Dogs even
used to come and lick his sores.
When the poor man died, he was

> carried away by angels to the bos-
> om of Abraham. The rich man also
> died and was buried, and from the
> netherworld, where he was in tor-
> ment, he raised his eyes and saw
> Abraham far off and Lazarus at his
> side. (Luke 16:20 23, NAB)

As I pulled into my office parking lot, I was approached by a man with a gasoline can.

"Hey man, can you help me with a few dollars for gas?" He asked. "No," I replied hurriedly, as I made my way into the office.

What he didn't know is that he had approached me three times with the same gas can story, and that he had been observed in our parking lot and a few of the nearby lots with the same story for the past month.

"It's his act," one fellow employee joked. "He must have found the gas can in a dumpster and came up with this story. And it must work because he has been using it for months!"

The following day at noon, I rushed out of the office to attend the 12:10 p.m. Mass at St. Bernard's. As I pulled into the parking lot, I spotted another man near the side door, soliciting money from mostly senior citizens going to Mass. Like the man the day before, I recognized him as a person that had "hit me up" for money on that same spot a while back. I was infuriated!

"Hey buddy, can you spare some money for a couple hamburgers, I haven't eaten in two days," was his pitch.

"No, I can't," I replied, raising my voice slightly. "I've seen you here before, and if you are hungry, like you say you are, then, you also know that there are at least five or six places where you can get a lunch, right now." The Haven of Rest, Salvation Army, Open M Pantry, Gennesaret, and Catholic Worker were a few that I quickly rattled off. "And you choose to stand here and take money from the very folks who support those organizations!" I concluded.

Embarrassed, he bowed his head and walked away, knowing that he had been dishonest and was discovered.

I share this story for two reasons.

First, since I work with the homeless, people often ask if they should give money to them. Many people are confused when they are approached as to whether they should offer help. Some have been burned in the past or have heard stories of people "scamming" the system. They see panhandlers on every freeway exit with their signs and are stopped as they go about their everyday activities.

"Are they really in need or are they just taking advantage of the poor economy to take money from unsuspecting folks?" they ask. The answer is not easy. I have been scammed, too many times to mention, often with the same sad story. It makes helping difficult! You just have to look at every instance and go with your intuition.

As I left church and made my way back to the car, I spotted the same gentleman leaning against a green dumpster.

"You give love a bad name!" I said, half serious and half smiling.

"You're right," he answered back as we got closer. And I want you to know that it won't happen again."

"Good," I exclaimed, as I gave him a firm hand shake, pressing a five-dollar bill into his hand. "Have a burger on me."

Reflection: *What did you do the last time you were asked for money on the street? Do you ever stop and give a donation to a panhandler on the freeway exit or street corner? How can you tell if the person is really in need or just a scam artist?*

The Sign of the Cross, That Thing You Do

> I, then, a prisoner for the Lord,
> urge you to live in a manner worthy
> of the call you have received, with
> all humility and gentleness, with pa-
> tience, bearing with one another
> through love. (Ephesians 4:1–2,
> NAB)

I noticed him as he walked into the classroom for our Catholic prayer service at the jail Tuesday night. He was smallish, meek, and had a very weak handshake. I also noticed that he seemed mentally slow.

About ten minutes into the service, he jumped to his feet and raising his hand above his head like a second grader, who knew the answer for the first time.

"Teach me to do that thing you do!" he exclaimed.

"What thing is that?" my friend George answered from the front of the classroom.

As the young man made a gesture with his hand on his forehead and chest and shoulders, George could see that he meant the sign of the cross.

"Do you mean the sign of the cross?" George asked.

"Yes! That's it; teach me the sign of the cross." was the inmate's response.

Patiently, as if he hadn't interrupted the prayer service, George made the sign of the cross as the inmate imitated his gestures.

"Do it again!" he said. And after each demonstration he would ask George to repeat it. It took around ten attempts until finally he had the gestures correct.

As the group began to grow impatient, he said to George, "Now teach me the words!" Again, with all the patience he could muster, understanding that the rest of the group was waiting to continue, George began, "In the name of the Father, and of the Son, and of the Holy Spirit, Amen."

The inmate repeated the words, slowly, over and over, until he finally got them correct. "Is this a prayer?" He asked.

"Yes, you could say that," George replied.

"I'm going to burn this into my mind," the inmate responded. Then he asked the most unusual question. "If I say this prayer a hundred times a day, would that be praying continuously, like Saint Paul said in that reading you just did?"

"I guess so. Yes, it would," was the reply.

"Then, that's what I am going to do! He exclaimed, as he sat back down in his seat.

You could see the sigh of relief as the service continued uninterrupted until the end. At the blessing, at the conclusion of the service, I couldn't help but notice the smile on his face as he traced the sign on his forehead, chest and shoulders and proudly spoke the words. And I also noticed, that the entire group of inmates, every one of them, Protestant, Catholic, atheists, and agnostics, all did the same.

I'll never look at the Sign of the Cross in the same way again. I've "burned it into my mind," along with this meek and humble inmate. After all, it's in the name of the Trinity that all prayer begins.

Reflection: *Do you often make the sign of the cross without giving it any thought? Does this inmate's excitement about the prayer inspire you?*

To Have a Father

We have become orphans, father-
less; widowed are our
mothers. (Lam 5:3, NAB)

As we sat on classroom chairs across from each other and began
to converse, I could tell that this was an intelligent young man.
Young, around 30, handsome and articulate, this is not the type of
person you would expect to meet in jail.

We talked about many things; faith, family, college, and politics. I
can't remember the exact conversation, but what I do remember
was when our time was up, he hugged me and said, "That must be
what it feels like to have a father!" Our conversation of fifteen
minutes or so was his first father-son talk, his first conversation
with a father figure, someone that he could admire.

"I wish we had more time, but tomorrow I'm being shipped out to
prison for 25 years," he said between tears.

Those words haunted me as I drove home from the jail that night:
that must be what it feels like to have a father. Through my tears I remembered that a huge percentage of men in prison have no
fathers, and if a man spends time in jail, the odds are better than
50 percent that his children will not have a father as well.

When I returned home, my wife was waiting up for me, reading
the newspaper on the couch in the family room. As I entered the
room and gave her a big "it's good to be home" kiss, she said,
"Did you read this story of a prisoner who raped a six-year-old
girl?"

After the night I had, I blurted out, "They better keep me away
from him, or I'll ring his neck!"

"They sentenced him to 25 years in prison," she answered back. With that, my wife went off to bed and I stayed behind, still needing some time to unwind from a long night at the jail.

I picked up the paper and read the article and realized that the prisoner she was talking about was the man I had just spoken with at the jail!

I can't begin to explain the feelings that were going through my mind, trying to make sense of this and finding no answers. I really began to feel that jail ministry was not for me.

A few weeks later, the incident still haunted me. I had a chance to have lunch with a good friend and psychologist, Dr. Ray, at an outdoor café in Naples, Florida. I shared this story with him.

"Tony, what do you call a six-year-old who is raped?" he asked.

"I'd call that child a victim!" I blurted out.

"And what do you call the person who commits such a crime?" Dr. Ray continued.

"A criminal," I responded.

And then he said something that still haunts me now, "Tony, they are the same person. I would bet you lunch that this man was abused as a child himself and since then, no one—not the system, a teacher, doctor, judge, or friend—has offered to get him help. There are two victims here."

When I returned to Ohio, I did some research and learned what Dr. Ray said was true. Not only was he abused himself, but he begged the system to get him help. They simply sentenced him to 25 years. He will be over 50 by the time he is released. If there is no help for him in prison, he will simply be returned to society with the same problems.

That was almost eight years ago. I'm still doing jail ministry, and not a day goes by that I don't offer up a prayer for that defenseless child and this young man. I still hear his trembling voice in my mind, "That must be what it feels like to have a father."

Note: Dr. Ray Guarendi is the father of ten, a clinical psychologist, author, public speaker, and nationally syndicated radio host. His radio show, *The Doctor Is In*, can be heard on EWTN.

Reflection: *As you read the story, did you pass judgement on this young man? Once you understood the circumstances, did it change the way you will approach judgement in the future?*

They Called Her Buffy

She was a pretty woman in her early forties, a homemaker, landscaper, and a former police officer who enjoyed drawing and the outdoors. That's what the obituary said. Buffy was also a heroin addict.

I got to know Buffy during the several months she was in jail. She was very likable and easy to talk with. She was looking forward to getting out of jail and on with her life, but as the time for release got nearer, she was concerned.

"I don't have any place I can go," she said. "I have nowhere to stay, and no one to help me."

"No one?" I asked. "Not a family member, a friend, or neighbor?"

"No," she replied, "no one."

We talked about an available halfway house or transitional housing unit, where she could stay until she got her bearings. There are very few resident houses available for women. According to a judge, who deals daily with the heroin epidemic, residential housing for women is one of the single most important needs for the county. Women with addictions have no chance if we send them back to a home in which a man is abusing drugs and alcohol every day.

Buffy assured me she would look into it, but I don't know that she did.

"I'll keep you in my prayers," I whispered as she gave me a hug at the end of our time together. That was the last time I saw her.

A week later, we were at a meeting of our jail ministry group when one of the members said to the group, "Did you hear about Buffy? She was released on Thursday and died of a heroin overdose on Sunday!"

Many thoughts raced through my mind. It seemed that, in reality, the jail had been keeping her alive, and with no one to help her on the outside, she simply returned to what she knew, heroin, and in three days, it killed her.

Did the system do enough for Buffy? Did the courts? Did we, as concerned citizens? Or worse yet, did I do enough? These questions will never be answered, but what I do know for sure is that she deserved help. How many other Buffy's are out there? Heroin is a powerful drug, and the odds of beating it are very slim, some say 3 percent. Tonight, say a prayer for Buffy and all the other Buffy's out there, that are hooked on this deadly drug. Pray that someday there might be easily available treatment and safe, transitional, residential facilities. If we only cared enough, it could happen.

Reflections: *Has heroin become a problem in your city or town? Has your picture of a heroin addict changed? Do you realize that it could be someone that looks just like you? Has your life been touched by a family member or friend's addiction?*

The Crosses We Bear

> God is faithful and will not let you
> be tried beyond your strength; but
> with the trial he will also provide a
> way out, so that you may be able to
> bear it. (1 Corinthians 10:13, NAB)

I was tired after a long day as the final group of inmates entered the classroom at the jail that evening. There were three men from the segregation pod. I shook hands with each of them as they entered the room.

"Please don't shake my hand too hard," one of the prisoners whispered, as I reached out my hand to greet him. "I have cancer and I'm in a lot of pain." As we took our seats, with Theresa, George, and me facing them, I said, "Tell me about your cancer."

He mentioned the long medical name for what type he had, and it is too long for me to remember, but he said that he had tumors in just about every organ in his body, all except his brain and lungs.

"What's the prognosis," I asked.

"A year to maybe three," was his response.

As we discussed his case, we learned that he had recently been convicted. He was told, however, that he would probably win an appeal. He said that he was innocent.

"How long does an appeal take?" I inquired.

"About a year," he said. "I might be dead before I am exonerated."

The second man offered that he was recently convicted and sentenced to twenty-five years to life. "I took a plea bargain," he offered. "I was facing multiple life sentences. I'll be sixty-three years old before I will come up for parole."

"You seem at peace with this." George questioned?

"Yes, I'm at peace, and I plan to use my time in prison to bring other men to Christ!"

When we turned to the third inmate, he swallowed hard and said, "I've been a jerk all my life, but today I am fifty days sober. I have traumatic stress syndrome. I've been shot in the head and out my neck. I have brain damage, deep depression, and mood swings."

"Wow," I thought, as I choked back tears. I can't think of three more difficult fates. One man is dying, another faces twenty-five to life in prison, and the third has brain damage and a lifetime of mental health issues. Of these three crosses to bear, which would I choose, if it had to be one of these?

"We would like to pray for you," I offered, not being able to think of anything we could say to ease their individual pain.

"Yes, that would be great," the dying prisoner replied.

Then, Theresa led us in prayer, and one by one we prayed for the inmate facing death. I was particularly moved by the prayer of the lifer. He felt that the dying man's fate was worse than his, and he prayed the most beautiful spirit-filled prayer.

One by one, we laid hands and prayed for each of the three men. Each made a statement that theirs was the easiest of the crosses to bear. Each felt more compassion for the others than the need for it themselves. It was a powerful reminder that each of us bears a cross as well, and only we can carry it.

It reminded me of the story of the man who prays to the Lord to "take this cross from me." Jesus takes the man into a room with crosses of all sizes, weights, and designs. As the man circles the room trying on cross after cross, he returns to the Lord and says,

"Jesus, I'll take this small one here." Jesus replies, "Sure, that's the same one you came in with."

Which of the three crosses would you choose? Or, would you rather keep the one you've got now? As for me, I'll keep mine, and continue to pray every day for those whose crosses would be too heavy for me to handle. These three men are carrying heavy crosses; please keep them in your prayers tonight.

Reflections: *Which of the three crosses would you choose? Or, would you rather keep the one you've got now? Are there those whose crosses would be too hard for you to handle?*

Took the Time

> Then the king will say to those on his right, "Come, you who are blessed by my Father. Inherit the kingdom prepared for you from the foundation of the world. For I was hungry, and you gave me food, I was thirsty, and you gave me drink, a stranger and you welcomed me, naked and you clothed me, ill and you cared for me, in prison and you visited me." (Matthew 25:34–36 NAB)

There is an old saying that roads are paved with good intentions, and in today's fast-paced, me-oriented society, it was never more evident. People are so consumed with their own lives, problems, and time that they barely have time to think of others.

Facebook has made the problem worse. It is an easy place to share your good intentions and an excuse not to do more. We respond to a post about a friend's health problems with "Thinking of you!" And that's it. You're done!

But what about going one step further? What about doing something more meaningful? What about putting service ahead of self?

A former co-worker in a city an hour away lost a parent. Most people didn't have time to make the one hour drive each way to attend. **But he did!**

The friend who just had major surgery at the hospital. Most people assumed she couldn't possibly want to see visitors, so they sent a Facebook message and were done. No one thought to visit her. **But she did!**

An elderly neighbor was dying and was sent to hospice for his final days. Sadly, no one visited him. **But he did.**

A homeless person was holding a sign, begging for money at the intersection while drivers waited for the light to turn green. No one reached into their pockets to help. **But she did.**

Who are these people that put service ahead of self? People that take time from their busy day to care for others, offer a kind word, visit people one-on-one.

They are the same people you will see at the adoration chapel, food pantry, and homeless shelter. They are the volunteers at the hospital, hospice, Salvation Army, or St. Vincent DePaul Society.

They are Christians, following the words of our Savior. They are living Matthew 25; not just posting nice thoughts on social media sites. They are involved, engaged, and making a difference.

When my father passed away, I remember one of his former fellow workers who flew in from Chicago to pay his respects. I remember him, **because he took the time.**

I remember everyone that visited me when I was in the hospital following cancer surgery. Everyone! And some were only casual friends and a few came a distance to visit. I remember them, **because they took the time.**

You probably have you own experience of the kindness of a friend, neighbor, or just someone who took the time to care. You remember them too, as I do, **because they took the time.**

These acts of kindness had an amazing effect on me. They were examples that helped me grow in my own faith journey. Never forget that just one act of kindness that you perform, may turn the tide of another person's life. The impact can be life changing!

Isn't that what we are all called to do?

On judgment day, when we stand before our Lord and are split into two groups, won't it be nice to hear Him welcome you into heaven knowing that when no one cared enough…**you did!**

Reflections: *Is there someone that you remember because of an act of kindness? Have you ever gone out of your way to help another? How did that make you feel?*

You Minister

Preach the Gospel at all times, and
when necessary, use words. (anonymous)

But you are "a chosen race, a royal
priesthood, a holy nation, a people
of his own, so that you may announce the praises" of him who
called you out of darkness into his
wonderful light. (1 Peter 2:9 NAB)

I've always been a fan of this quote often attributed wrongly to St.
Francis. It speaks volumes about ministry. As Catholics, we typi-
cally refer to the word ministry as something done by the ordained.
And we use the word apostolate for laymen.

But semantics aside, all of us have a ministry. We are all called by
Jesus to minister to each other, to preach the gospel always.

Last week, I exchanged posts with a friend in Ireland who had
been in full-time ministry, but currently isn't.

"I always thought that I would spend the rest of my life in full-
time ministry," he said.

"But you are in full-time ministry," I offered. "You minister every
day, twenty-four hours a day."

You minister by the way you treat your spouse and honor your
Christ-centered marriage.

You minister by the way you love your children. Kids are always watching, modelling, and listening to how their parents
handle issues. Early in their lives, they will know what role faith
plays in their parents' lives.

You minister to your friends, by the little things you do, and how you are there for them when times are tough.

You minister to people at work by how you conduct business and how you treat customers or clients.

You minister to your community by how you involve yourself in your church, in charitable causes, and civic issues.

When I was a young father in a new town, I looked to the older men of my parish as examples. I watched the way they treated their wives, families, and fellow parishioners. I imitated them. Many of them became friends.

I am aware that younger men are watching me as well. I need to be the same example of Christ's love to them, as those older parishioners were for me. After all, I'm ministering.

When the elderly man patiently helps his wife shuffle to her pew with a walker before Mass—he is ministering.

When the woman leads her husband, who suffered a stroke, up the aisle to receive communion—she is ministering.

When the mother helps her mentally handicapped child with the Sign of the Cross—she is ministering.

When the altar boys, lectors, choir members, and others stay after morning Mass on Friday to clean the church for the weekend— they are ministering.

Yes, you minister. You minister by your actions; by the way you treat people. You minister by the way you love your spouse, family, and friends. You minister by the way you conduct your business.

We are all called by Our Lord to go and make disciples of those we meet, and by our example bring them into an understanding of our faith. We are called to live the faith by our words and actions. We are called to be an example of what it looks like to be a Christian.

And occasionally, when necessary, we might even need to use words!

Reflections: What do you do in your daily life that you would consider ministry? Have you ever considered that the way you treat people is part of your ministry? How do others minister to you?

A Giving Heart

> When he looked up he saw some wealthy people putting their offerings into the treasury and he noticed a poor widow putting in two small coins. He said, "I tell you truly, this poor widow put in more than all the rest; for those others have all made offerings from their surplus wealth, but she, from her poverty, has offered her whole livelihood." (Luke 21:1–4 NAB)

About fifty years ago, a young girl was moved by the request of her preacher a few weeks before Christmas. The preacher mentioned from the pulpit that there was a family in their very small congregation that was down on their luck. The father was unemployed, the oldest child was ill, and every penny they had could hardly keep the family together.

"Wouldn't it be nice," he offered, "if the congregation would all bring in what they could next Sunday and present it to this wonderful family."

The young girl was determined to do whatever she could that week to bring in any money she could accumulate to help them.

She tapped her piggy bank; she looked for loose change in the sofa cushions and helped a neighbor with some chores to earn another dollar. All in all, she accumulated $2.73.

The next Sunday, as she walked down the center aisle to drop her $2.73 in the basket, she felt humble; embarrassed that she could only give this needy family less than $3.

At the end of the service, the preacher called the family up to the front to present the money that the congregation had collected. To the young girl's amazement, it was her family!

I heard about this story from that same young girl, fifty years later, after becoming a successful business woman. She told the story from a banquet podium the night she was honored for her philanthropy.

Her story reminded me of the poor widow's two small coins. She was generous even though she had very little to give.

To me, this story proves one thing: that generosity has nothing to do with a person's financial situation. A generous person is generous whether they are rich or poor.

In my experience, some of the most generous people I ever met were people with very limited means. They give out of the kindness of their hearts. They give to be a blessing. They give out of a sense of gratitude, and they work so that they can have a chance to give. They realize that it is impossible to love without giving.

They truly have the heart of a giver. They realize that giving increases their happiness. They don't give to get. They have no selfish motives. They often give anonymously, so as not to draw attention to themselves.

If I asked who are the most Christ-like people you know, many would say their grandma, their mom, a special aunt, their father or grandfather because those people have generous hearts.

What can we do to have a giving heart? We can start by counting our blessings. Gratitude leads to generosity when we realize, no matter our circumstances, someone is suffering more.

Let's make it a goal to have a giving heart!

Reflections: *Who are the most Christ-like people you know? Do you believe that generosity has little to do with the amount of money involved? How do we measure our generosity?*

Good People, Bad Choices

As he continued his journey to Jerusalem, he traveled through Samaria and Galilee. As he was entering a village, ten lepers met [him]. They stood at a distance from him and raised their voice, saying, "Jesus, Master! Have pity on us!" And when he saw them, he said, "Go show yourselves to the priests." As they were going they were cleansed. And one of them, realizing he had been healed, returned, glorifying God in a loud voice; and he fell at the feet of Jesus and thanked him. He was a Samaritan. Jesus said in reply, "Ten were cleansed, were they not? Where are the other nine? Has none but this foreigner returned to give thanks to

God?" Then he said to him, "Stand
up and go; your faith has saved
you." (Luke 17:11–19, NAB)

In almost eight years of jail ministry, I am often asked, "What kind
of people do you meet in jail?" My response is usually, "I meet
good people that have made some very bad choices."

Most of the inmates that I work with in jail are good people who
made some of the worst choices. They really lack the decision-
making skills to make smart choices.

This week we had three inmates who lost loved ones to drugs in
the recent past. One woman told of how her boyfriend "took his
last breath in her arms." A second woman had lost an aunt to
heroin. And a man had lost his wife to crystal meth. All were in jail
on their own drug charges.

You would think that watching a boyfriend die in your arms or
losing an aunt to drugs would cause you to examine your own life,
your own addictions, and decide to get help. Unfortunately, that's
not the case. The bad decisions just continue forward.

And what I have witnessed is that one bad decision usually leads to
another and the effect can be devastating.

Those bad decisions land you in jail. Like the lepers in Luke's gospel, you feel alone, ostracized, set apart from society, surrounded
by others who have made similar bad decisions. What can they do?

In Luke's gospel, three things happened to the Samaritan.

1. He recognized he had a problem and was helpless to solve
    it alone. He needed help from a higher power. He needed
    God's help!
2. He prayed for that assistance, "Jesus have pity on me."
    And the Lord cured him.

3. He offered thanks for the miracle he received. Unlike the other nine, he returned to Jesus and thanked him. He expressed gratitude.

Can I ask you a question? What is your leprosy?

I don't mean a skin disorder; I mean what is the thing that separates you from God and from others? For many of the inmates I see, it is heroin, meth, alcohol, crack cocaine, pornography.

Yours may not be drugs or alcohol, but we all have our own personal leprosy, that one sin or one bad habit that keeps us from a relationship with our Lord.

Once we realize that we can't handle it alone and need God's help, we need to call on him for help through prayer. A simple morning prayer I suggest to addicts is, "Lord, help me get through this day," a day without drugs or alcohol or pornography. And a simple evening prayer is, "Lord, thank you for your help this day."

One day at a time, one good decision at a time, we learn to become better decision makers. We never bat 1,000, but then, major league baseball's batting champion doesn't either. He just has a good batting average. And you can improve yours with prayer.

Ultimately, our lives are the sum total of the choices we make. Let's prayerfully choose wisely.

Reflection: *Have you ever been haunted by the bad choices you made? How can we make better choices in the future?*

From Darkness Toward the Light

> To open their eyes that they may
> turn from darkness to light and
> from the power of Satan to God, so
> that they may obtain forgiveness of
> sins and an inheritance among
> those who have been consecrated
> by faith in me. (Acts 26:18, NAB)

In jail ministry, we see a lot of people whose lives have been forever altered by drugs and alcohol. Their addiction causes them to make life choices that lead them to stealing, robbery, selling drugs, burglary, breaking and entering, and many other bad life choices. They do this to get the drugs or booze they need to make them "feel good."

How is that working for you? Not very well, many answer. Their lives are going nowhere and only a complete turn-around will save them from imprisonment.

The word for a complete turnaround in Greek is *metanoia*. Real repentance involves this 180-degree turn-around. I often say it is moving toward the light (God) and away from darkness (the devil).

If the direction we are going, the friends we have, and the addictions we embrace are taking us in the direction of darkness, and the result is winding up in a jail cell, then no matter how good we think the drugs or alcohol make us feel, it isn't working!

If we beat our heads against the same wall, at some point we have to turn left or right, or turn around to stop the pain, permanently.

Moving toward the light and away from darkness involves two steps:

First, we must understand that the current direction isn't working. It is a dead-end street to pain, misery, and unhappiness.

Second, we must ask for God's help. We need to understand that we are not capable of overcoming these addictions ourselves. It takes divine intervention; a higher power. It takes God's help. We must humbly pray for God's mercy.

Often, I suggest the simple prayer, "Lord, get me through this day (today)." One day at a time, with God's help, we can change our lives. We can have a *metanoia*. We can have true repentance. We can move toward the light and away from darkness, away from a world blocked with our own shadow, and into the light that is the tender presence of our Lord.

Reflection: Do you sometimes feel you are moving toward darkness instead of light? What does it take to make the turnaround? Have you ever had to change directions in your life?

How Do You Eat an Elephant?

> What is born of human nature is
> human; what is born of the Spirit is
> spirit. Do not be surprised when I
> say: You must be born from above.
> (1 John 3:6-7, NAB)

Most of the people I see who are incarcerated in local jails have one thing in common: drug and alcohol abuse. No matter what crime they have committed, the underlying problem is usually drugs, alcohol, or both.

Whenever I speak to a group in jail, I like to ask a silly question.

"How do you eat an elephant?" I'll exclaim.

After a few weird looks, a long moment of silence, and a few muf-fled laughs, I'll answer my own question. "You eat it one bite at a time, one forkful at a time, or spoonful at a time!"

After a few more seconds of silence, I'll ask one of the inmates, "What is your elephant?"

"Heroin," he'll reply with an embarrassing look on his face.

"And how are you going to eat this elephant?" I probe.

Then, as if a light bulb appears above his head, he replies, "One day at a time!"

"You've got it!" I'll excitedly confirm. "You win the battle against drugs one day at a time. For some, it's more difficult. It's one hour at a time, or one minute at a time. You can't do it alone. You need a higher power. You need God to help you."

You know the same holds true for all of us. We all face our own personal elephants! Sickness, disease, a bad marriage, financial dif-ficulties, a job loss—they all seem like problems that are too big for us to handle.

Truthfully, if we try to beat them ourselves, then they are too big to handle! But with God's help, we can break down these chal-lenges into bite-sized forkfuls. The Holy Spirit will guide us if we call upon His help.

> No trial has come to you but what is human. God is faithful and will not let you be tried beyond your strength; but with the trial he will also provide a way out, so that you may be able to bear it. (1 Corinthi-ans 10:13, NAB)

1 Cor. 10:13 doesn't imply that we won't have problems, but it does say that if you remain faithful, as God is faithful, he will pro-

vide for you a way out, so that the problem will be bearable. Not alone, but with God's help, this is possible.

Let me ask you, "What is your elephant?"

Reflection: *What is your elephant and how are you going to deal with it one day at a time?*

This was a Night to Pray

> Persevere in prayer, being watchful in it with thanksgiving; at the same time pray for us, too, that God may open a door to us for the word, to speak of the mystery of Christ, for which I am in prison. (Colossians 4:2–3, NAB)

As the women entered the classroom for our Tuesday night prayer service at the jail, I noticed that many of them had been crying. As the service began, one of the women interrupted and asked if we could pray for Heather back in the female pod. Heather had just received word that her five-year-old son, Matthew, had been killed in an automobile accident with a foster family.

Losing a child has to be one of the most devastating experiences a parent could face, but the thought of being in jail and having a child die while in foster care would be unbearable. As we began to pray for Heather and Matthew, the door of the classroom opened and one of the guards asked if there was someone who could speak with Heather. Deacon Roger left with the guard to minister to her as the service continued.

I can't remember much about the service, except that everyone was attentive and prayerful.

As we finished the service, the back doors of the classroom opened, and there was Deacon Roger along with Heather. Immediately, without any discussion, everyone jumped to their feet and went to their sobbing fellow inmate.

Amid the tears, I asked if we could all pray for her and her son, Matthew. The twelve women in orange jumpsuits and our ministry team laid hands on Heather. We prayed for her and her son. It was a moving experience!

You see, even in jail, God calls us to be a light for others. If all of our freedoms are taken away, we can still pray and be a blessing to those around us. We talk about this often at the jail, and you might be surprised how many inmates take this to heart.

At every service, we offer a chance for intercessions, and the inmates respond with prayer requests for parents, grandparents, children and other inmates. They even pray for the success of our ministry. You know, the prayers of prisoners are very powerful. Need proof? Just look at what the Apostle Paul accomplished with prayer while he was in prison.

Reflection: *Have you ever dropped what you were doing to pray? How has spontaneous prayer changed your life?*

Bad Company

> Do not be led astray: "*Bad Company* corrupts good morals." (1 Corinthians 15:33, NAB; emphasis added)

My dad had a simple philosophy: "You are who you hang out with!" He would argue that if you hung out with complainers, you became a complainer. If you hung out with drinkers, you would become a drinker. If your friends did drugs, eventually you would too.

The other evening, at a men's prayer group, one of the guys said, "Wow! It is really great hanging out with a group of like-minded Christians!" I agreed.

If Paul's statement about bad company corrupting good morals is true, then it makes sense that good company reinforces good morals.

Why is it, then, that we choose to associate with the wrong people?

I recall an incident from a few years ago, at the jail, where a young woman who had served time for drugs was being released. In the parking lot of the jail were two different cars with people that had come to pick her up. In one car were her parents, in the other her drug friends. These were the same friends that she was hanging out with when she was arrested months earlier.

Which group did she choose—her parents or friends? You guessed it; she got into the car with her friends! Three days later she was back in jail facing another drug charge, this one with an even greater consequence.

In my many years ministering to the incarcerated, I met very few bad people. There are some, to be sure. But most of them are good people, who simply made bad choices. Often, the best thing they can do when they are released is to make some new friends; good friends, positive friends.

In Acts 19, the Apostle Paul entered Ephesus and found only twelve men who believed in Jesus, and after baptizing them in Christ's name, spent the next two years discussing Jesus with anyone who would listen. Remarkably, in just two years, all the inhabitants of the province of Asia had heard the Word of the Lord, without Facebook or Twitter!

With whom do you spend the most time? Is our Lord at the top of that list? Does he even make the top ten? Try to spend time with the people that lift you up, challenge you to be better, do more, care more, love more, and pray more.

Growing up, I found myself attracted to people who were positive, caring, and had a close relationship with God. I walked away from many conversations with fellow students or workers that were negative or unproductive. I think Dad's simple philosophy had a big effect on me: "Whom you associate with is what you will become."

Reflections: What do you think of the comment, "Whom you associate with is what you will become?" Change your friends, change your outcome. Do you agree? Do you spend time with the Lord in prayer?

Walk Your Talk

"For I was hungry, and you gave me food, I was thirsty and you gave me drink, a stranger and you welcomed me, naked and you clothed me, ill and you cared for me, in prison and you visited me." Then the righteous will answer him and say, "Lord, when did we see you hungry and feed you, or thirsty and give you drink? When did we see you a stranger and welcome you, or naked and clothe you? When did we see you ill or in prison, and visit you?" And the king will say to them in reply, "Amen, I say to you, whatever you did for one of these least

brothers of mine, you did for me."
(Matthew 25:35–40, NAB)

In his homily this past Sunday, Father Mike used the phrase, "Put feet under your faith." I smiled. I hadn't heard that phrase since the late 1970's.

It's a phrase that we used when we discussed putting our faith in action, to reach out to those less fortunate and offer a helping hand. We would ask, "You can talk the talk; can you walk the talk?"

Too often, Christians spend a lot of time talking. We talk about how we have been saved, how blessed we are, how much we love Jesus, and what our faith means to us, but we never put this talk into action.

Mahatma Gandhi said, "The best way to find yourself is to lose yourself in the service of others."[5]

And it's true! There is something very therapeutic about serving others. There is real power in service! Serving others can cure many ills.

Are you suffering from low self-esteem? Try feeding the hungry.

Feeling anger or resentment? Try volunteering at a homeless shelter.

Do you feel like you're a failure? Try working with the mentally or physically handicapped.

For the Son of Man did not come
to be served, but to serve and to
give his life as a ransom for many.
(Mark 10:45, NAB).

When we show concern for others, our own health will likely improve. Caring for others will make you more joyful and grateful, and you will view life with new clarity.

In Matthew 25, we read the only description in the Bible of the last judgment. Feed the hungry, clothe the naked, care for the ill, welcome strangers—all of which involve walking the walk and practicing what we preach.

In the book *The Power of Serving Others,* [6] authors Gary Morsch and Dean Nelson teach us:

1. Everyone has something to give.
2. Most people are willing to give when they see the need and have the opportunity.
3. Everyone can do something for someone right now.

Don't wait to be asked. We need to be open to those opportunities to put our faith in action as they present themselves. We all have gifts; things that we do well. It can be anything from teaching to swinging a hammer; from mowing a neighbor's lawn to cooking a meal for an elderly friend. There are ways to use our gifts for the service of others.

Isn't it time we started to walk our talk and to practice what we preach?

It's time to put feet under our faith!

Reflection: *How are you walking your talk? Are you putting you faith into action? What can you do to put your talents to work for the betterment of others?*

CHAPTER TWO

God s Grace in Taking Action

The Three O'clock Call

> Now when three of Job's friends
> heard of all the misfortune that had
> come upon him, they set out each
> one from his own place: Eliphaz
> from Teman, Bildad from Shuh,
> and Zophar from Naamath. They
> met and journeyed together to give
> him sympathy and comfort. (Job
> 2:11, NAB)

Years ago, working at a radio station in Cleveland, I met Rena. Rena was an energetic, dynamic, community affairs director who whipped cancer twice. It takes a strong person to beat the odds against cancer and do it not once but twice.

What does a two-time cancer survivor do? Make a three o'clock call!

Every day at three, Rena would drop everything she was doing and make a telephone call to someone in need. It might be someone in the hospital, or someone who was at home, sick. It could be someone that had just been diagnosed with an illness, or a person that had lost a spouse, or someone who was going through a divorce or rough patch.

The purpose of the call was simple. Just to let someone know that she was thinking of them, supported them, and loved them -every day at three, without fail.

I remember asking her once, if she ever ran out of people to call. "Never, there are always people that we know who are in need," she replied. And she was right.

Several years later, I decided I was going to carry on her three o'clock tradition. And for a while, I did. Everyone I called said, "You know, I was just thinking of you," or "It's so great to hear your voice." And everyone was thankful for the call.

As time passed, so did my diligence to the call, but recently I've started again. Think about it; you might want to join me.

Reflections: Have you ever made a call to someone and they said they were just thinking of you? Do you occasionally call old friends to check in? When someone is in the hospital or recovering at home, do you check in?

Pray for Me Now!

> Again, (amen,) I say to you, if two
> of you agree on earth about any-
> thing for which they are to pray, it
> shall be granted to them by my
> heavenly Father. (Matthew 18:19,
> NAB)

If you are like me, as you go about your day, someone will share a story, a problem, an injury, or bad diagnosis with you. If you show concern, as I do, they will often ask you to pray for them.

Until recently, I would respond, "Of course I will."

Then, when I returned home, I added their name to the prayer list that I keep on my nightstand.

I recently realized, after a lively discussion on the topic with my breakfast buddies, that this isn't what the person asked. She didn't say to go home and write me on your prayer list. She said, "Pray for me!" As in NOW!

Nowhere in the Bible do I remember Jesus saying that he would pray later. On the contrary, He would drop everything else he was doing and would pray right then and there, being totally attentive to the person in front of him.

That's an example we all need to follow, whether at the grocery store, at lunch, or at a ball game. If someone asks us to pray for them, let's do it *right now!*

Reflections: *Have you ever stopped what you were doing to pray for some-one? Did you find that experience positive? Was the other person apprehensive or welcoming?*

Lord, Show Me a Sign, Hit Me Over the Head

> God added his testimony by signs,
> wonders, various acts of power, and
> distribution of the gifts of the holy
> Spirit according to his will. (He-
> brews 2:4, NAB)

To say I wasn't having a good day would be an understatement. Nothing, from the time I opened my eyes, was going right. As I drove to work, I prayed my favorite prayer: "Lord make me an instrument; put someone in front of me today that you can help through me." Only this time I added, "And by the way, Lord, the way things are going today, you'll probably have to hit me over the head to get my attention, if you expect anything from me."

During my lunch hour, I stopped at my bank to pay a bill with a small expense check. As I waited in line at the teller's window, I couldn't help but overhear a conversation going on at the next window. A young woman was paying her mortgage, but her checking account was two dollars short and she didn't have any cash with her. "It's a shame that you will have to go back home to get two dollars," the teller said, "but there isn't anything I can do."

It was my turn in line, and as I hurriedly handed over the transaction to my teller, I was too focused on my own bad day to realize that two dollars was my exact change!

I thanked the teller and without giving it another thought rushed back to my car. As I opened the door to get in, the sun visor fell hitting me right on the forehead! It wasn't loose, or broken, and this had never happened before, but it hurt. "Ouch!" I yelled in a loud voice.

Then, I remembered. I had asked God to hit me over the head to get my attention, if he needed me that day. Immediately I returned to the bank and handed the young woman the two dollars she needed. She smiled and gave me a hug, as the teller happily completed her transaction.

As I returned to work, I couldn't help but think that my day was going to get better, except, that is, for the lump on my forehead. And to tell the truth, it did. God has an unusual sense of humor.

Reflection: *Has God ever hit you over the head to get your attention?*

Two Dollars and a Bus Pass

> When he looked up he saw some wealthy people putting their offerings into the treasury and he noticed a widow putting in two small coins. He said, "I tell you truly, this poor woman put in more than all the rest; for those others have all made offerings from their surplus wealth, but she, from her poverty, has offered her whole livelihood." (Luke 21:1–4, NAB)

As I left the 12:10 Mass at St. Bernard's on a cold winter day and headed back to the office, I decided to stop at the local Arby's for a roast beef sandwich and a Coke. Although it wasn't yet one o'clock, the restaurant was nearly empty, and I was the only person in line.

As I approached the cashier, I could tell that she had been crying. Her eyes were red, and she held back the sniffles that accompanied her sadness. As I waited for my food, another worker came over to console her friend. I couldn't help but overhear some of their conversation. The crying girl was broke, and there were still two days until pay day. She had no food or bus pass. I was amazed when her young friend made her a generous offer. "I have two dollars and a bus pass," she said. "I'll happily give you the money and keep the bus pass or give you the pass and keep the two dollars."

Now that's generosity, I thought. It reminded me of the poor widow's mite in the gospels of Mark and Luke. As I reached into my wallet, all I had were two twenty-dollar bills. I hesitated for a moment and handed each of them $20 and told them it was a tip for their good service.

Dumbfounded, they accepted the money, and as I left I could see them in the reflection of the window giving each other a tearful hug. Forty dollars didn't seem like much compared to two dollars or a bus pass.

Reflections: *What can we learn from the poor widow in the gospels? Do you find that the people who have little are more inclined to share what they have than people with more? The young girl didn't have much, but she offered to share what little she had. Have you ever been in this position? How did you react?*

It's a Matter of Trust

> So now, my son, find yourself a
> trustworthy man who will make the
> journey with you. (Tobit 5:3, NAB)

As I sat waiting for Sunday Mass to begin, I felt a tap on my shoulder. In the aisle was an older woman who politely asked, "Are you Tony?"

"Yes," I replied.

"And you work with Living Bread Radio, right?" she questioned.

"Yes, I do," I responded.

Just then she pressed a wad of bills into my hand and asked if I could deliver her donation to the radio station. "Sure," I replied, "but I won't be there for a couple of weeks."

"That's OK," she calmly replied.

As I took the money from her hand, I asked her if I could get a name and address so that the station could send her a thank you note.

"No, that's alright, I prefer to remain anonymous," she said quietly, "and I trust you!"

As she walked back to her seat, I couldn't help but think, "She trusts me, and she doesn't even know me. I could simply take the money, and no one would know. Yet, she trusts me! If you take one look at me, I look like a poster boy for the movie *Goodfellas*, yet she *trusts* me.

The next day, I made my way to Indiana to see a client. After four and a half hours in the car, tired and hungry, I stopped at a service station for some $4 per gallon gasoline! As I pumped gas into my guzzling SUV, a late 1980's Buick pulled up to the pump next to me. An elderly man got out of the car and immediately approached me.

"Excuse me, but I was visiting my friend in the hospital and realized as I pulled in to the gas station that I left my wallet at my home in Bloomington. I don't have any cash and my car is on empty."

"Oh, boy," I thought, and then asked, "Why did you ask me when there are so many other people at the pumps?"

"Because you look like I could trust you," he replied.

"Really?! All of these people and you think I look trustworthy?" I inquired with disbelief animated on my face.

"Yes, I had a feeling that I could ask you and you would help me," he said in a soft voice.

Well, I knew that he trusted me, but did I trust him? This wasn't the first time I'd heard this very story at a gas station. As a matter of fact, there were two different times in the past month that I had been approached and I turned both requests down. But not this time!

"Well," I said. I trust you too, as I swiped my credit card to get him enough gas to get back home.

Did I trust him because he was an elderly farmer in a Buick? Would I have trusted him if he were younger or an African-American? Or did I trust him because the day before a woman I didn't know trusted me with a large amount of cash?

I'll have to think more about that. Maybe God is telling me something about trust, but I can tell you that it felt good to help him and even better to be trusted by the woman at church.

I never imagined that I looked trustworthy!

Reflections: *Do people trust you? Why would you trust a stranger?*

Jesus, Take the Wheel

He who plans a thing will be successful; happy is he who trusts in the Lord! (Proverbs 16:20, NAB)

But he who trusts in the Lord will
prosper. (Proverbs 28:25, NAB)

The fear of man brings a snare, but
he who trusts in the Lord is
safe. (Proverbs 29:25, NAB)

As we made our way down Interstate 77 on our annual vacation trip to Florida, everything was going as planned. We had just finished a nice dinner in Charlotte and we were making our way to Orangeburg, South Carolina, for the night. With light traffic, the radio playing the local country station, I was totally in control, just the way I like it.

Then, my navigation screen flashed, the car slowed to forty mph, and the message on the navigation system read, "Powering Down, Seek Service Immediately!"

"What the #$@&!," I exclaimed.

Just then, the car powered down to twenty mph, and with the traffic that night going 75 to 80, it was time to pull over to the side of the road. Our perfectly timed trip, planned for weeks, was now out of my hands, and I didn't like it. I could feel my temper flaring; I was angry and out of control.

As I pulled over to the side of the road, Carrie Underwood was singing her hit song, *Jesus, Take the Wheel.* As she belted out the line, I had a flashback to when I had been diagnosed with cancer eight years earlier. I wasn't in control of that situation. I was poked and prodded by doctors and nurses, and I really didn't have much say in what was going to happen. I had to trust in the Lord, and let Jesus take the wheel. At that moment, I decided this situation required doing the same thing. "Jesus," I prayed, "please help us."

The sequence of events that happened next was nothing short of divine intervention. The state highway patrolman happened to know a tow truck driver that lived less than 5 minutes away. He was willing to come down and tow us to the nearest dealership, 40 miles away in the small town of Winnsboro, South Carolina. The dealership was small, but Susan, in the service department was amazing. She was able to get James, a local gentleman, to drive us to Columbia, South Carolina to get a rental car. The computer part we needed would take several days to get and install. Then James would pick us up again, to return to the dealership, to get our car at the end of our vacation.

By letting Jesus take the wheel, there is no telling what this delay might have prevented. Perhaps there was a major accident that we avoided. Maybe breaking down in the mountains of Virginia or West Virginia would have been a disaster. Maybe this was supposed to happen just the way it did. Maybe the Lord was really looking out for us. We will never know.

What I do know is that as much as I am a control freak and I want everything to go as planned, in reality, I am not in control! When I realize that everything is in God's hands and I simply trust in him, things seem to work out better. The more I learn to trust in him, the better my life gets. Maybe the cancer surgery helped to make this point in a way that even a control freak could understand.

Now, when things seem out of my control, I simply ask Jesus to take the wheel! *Jesus, I trust in you.*

Reflections: *Have you ever thought you were in complete control and found out you weren't? Have you ever been in such a tough situation that you simply had to turn things over to the Lord? Is it difficult for you to give up control?*

Is Mario Andretti My Guardian Angel?

For he commands his angels with regard to you, to guard you wherever you go. (Psalm 91:11, NAB)

Today is the feast of the Guardian Angels, and I am a big fan of my Guardian Angel, Mario. I've been praying the Guardian Angel prayer since I was a little kid and do so every day. It was 9 years ago when I discovered my Guardian Angel's name.

I was on a business trip to Lansing, Michigan, a trip I have made over a hundred times in the past ten years. On this trip, I was heading north on Interstate 69, between Jackson and Lansing, when a tractor-trailer rig passed me like I was standing still. As the truck passed, he immediately started pulling into my lane and I quickly realized that his trailer was going to hit me, or worse, drive me off the road.

I hit my brakes and veered to the right to avoid a collision, but as I did, I hit some gravel in the berm and started to spin out.

My SUV made three complete revolutions, crossing from the right lane to the left lane and back again, barely missing several vehicles on the busy highway.

Everything seemed to move in slow motion. I realized that someone else was guiding the steering wheel. Finally, I came to rest in the center island, facing oncoming traffic, completely stopped. There wasn't a scratch on me or my SUV. Papers from my passenger seat littered the floor of the car.

When the nightmare was over, I prayed, "Thank you, Lord for guiding me through this without anyone getting injured." I know that my Guardian Angel was in control, because even Mario Andretti couldn't escape what happened without a serious accident!

From that day forward, my Guardian Angel was Mario! Now when I pray the Guardian Angel prayer, I include him:

> Angel of God, My Guardian Dear
> To whom God's love commits me
> here.
> Ever this day be at my side
> To light and guard and rule and

guide.
P.S. Mario, keep me safe today!
Amen

I read recently that the Church doesn't recommend naming your Guardian Angel. Although, I can't understand why.

Unless, of course, when I finally meet my Guardian Angel in heaven and we embrace in a big man-hug, he looks at me and says, "Tony!" And I enthusiastically reply, "Mario!"

Then he says, "Uh, Tony, I've been meaning to talk with you about that, my name isn't Mario."

Embarrassed by this realization, I respond, "I am so sorry for calling you by the wrong name all of these years. Tell me, what is your name?"

With a smile bigger than life he replies, "Dale Junior!"

Reflections: Do you believe in guardian angels? Have you ever felt that your guardian angel was with you in a tough situation? Do you ever speak to your guardian angel?

The 80 MPH Rosary

Persevere in prayer, being watchful
in it with thanksgiving. (Colossians
4:2, NAB)

Most traveling salesmen can tell you, it gets mighty boring traveling for hours in the car. On the way home from a recent trip, I was bored to tears with every radio station on the dial. I tried seek/scan, AM, FM, XM, but nothing seemed to keep my attention.

As I merged onto I-275 around Cincinnati, a balding, chubby guy in a Mercedes Benz passed me as if I was standing still. That guy had to be going 80! As he passed, I noticed a rosary draped over his steering wheel as he fingered the beads.

"That's it," I thought. "I'll pray the rosary too!"

I reached into my glove compartment, got out my rosary and draped it over the steering wheel. I began to pray as I pulled into the passing lane and sped up until I was right behind the Benz!

I think he spotted my rosary, and as we prayed we made the quickest loop around Cincinnati ever. (Now, I am not advocating speeding, but I have never been pulled over while praying the rosary...*just saying.*)

As we finished the rosary, I saw the man in the Benz put on his blinker, heading for the exit; one exit before mine. As he slowed down approaching the exit, we were again side by side and made the sign of the cross together! He smiled and nodded, and I smiled back.

Moments later, I reached my exit. As I exited, the Catholic radio station was airing the Chaplet of Divine Mercy, the one with the singing nuns that I really like, so, since my rosary was already in my hands, I prayed along.

Boredom curbed, at least for the moment, three hours of driving remained. I slowed down to the speed limit and relaxed with my rosary in hand.

Next time you are driving and bored, try praying a rosary—at the speed limit!

Reflection: Have you ever prayed a rosary when you were bored? Did it help relieve the stir-crazy feeling? Is the car a great place to pray the rosary? Do you have a prayer life in the car?

It Takes a Licking and Keeps on Ticking

> Or what woman having ten coins
> and losing one would not light a
> lamp and sweep the house, search-
> ing carefully until she finds it? And
> when she does find it, she calls to-
> gether her friends and neighbors
> and says to them, "Rejoice with me
> because I have found the coin that
> I lost." In just the same way, I tell
> you, there will be rejoicing among
> the angels of God over one sinner
> who repents. (Luke 15:8–10, NAB)

It was dark as we made our way to the parking lot following a recent board meeting in Cleveland. As I got to my car, I wanted to
remove my sport coat to be comfortable for the long ride home.

After setting my iPad on the hood of my car, I removed my coat,
opened the back door of my SUV, and hung the coat neatly on a
hanger.

I returned and said my goodbyes to the group, entered the vehicle
and made my way down the main street for several blocks. I drove
the short distance to the entrance ramp for the highway. As I
made my way up the ramp, I accelerated to get up to the speed
limit as I merged.

As I accelerated, I noticed what looked like a leather case about
the size of an iPad flying over my windshield, over the roof of the
car. As I glanced into my rear-view mirror, all I could see was this
object, at least ten feet in the air, disappear into the darkness behind me.

"Oh my, it's my iPad," I realized. "I forgot I left it on the hood!" I was nauseated.

I hurriedly got off on at the next exit, stopped my car and searched the back seat of my car, even though I knew I wouldn't find it. Making a U-turn, I got back on the highway and made my way back to where I saw the flying iPad.

As I retraced my route, I began to pray to St. Anthony, the patron saint of lost articles. I pray the St. Anthony prayer often, but in my panic, I couldn't remember. All I could remember was the simple little prayer that we were taught as children.

Tony, Tony look around,

Help me find what can't be found.

As I approached the interstate ramp, I turned on my bright lights and emergency flashers and slowly made my way up the ramp. It was very dark and there were weeds three feet high on both sides of the road. As I neared the top of the ramp, I saw a street light. It was shining like a spotlight at a rock concert on a small area of the berm, and there lay my iPad!

I opened the door and scooped it off the blacktop and threw it on to my passenger seat, then quickly sped up to allow the other cars to enter the ramp.

As I made my way home, thanking God (and St. Anthony) for finding my iPad, with all of my personal data, prayers, notes for my book, e-mails and business information, I reached over to the passenger seat and pushed the button to turn on my device. It lit up and was working fine, except for the shattered screen.

I wish I could have prayed a more adult prayer, but it seems that St. Anthony liked this one just fine!

Reflections: Have you ever prayed to find a lost object? Did it work? Did you learn the prayer to St. Anthony and have you used it?

We Never Forget Kindness

Give, and gifts will be given to you;
a good measure, packed together,
shaken down, and overflowing, will
be poured into your lap. For the
measure with which you measure
will in return be measured out to
you. (Luke 6:38, NAB)

There is something wonderful about kindness. We remember for years kindnesses that we received, many unexpectedly, some a needed blessing, others true miracles. Kindness is not easily forgotten.

When you look back over the years, there are always small acts of kindness that you never forget; random acts of kindness, often from strangers, that were God sent.

The woman who lost her husband in an automobile accident will never forget the five hundred-dollar anonymous check she received in the mail to help with that month's rent.

The unemployed parents wondering how they will ever afford Christmas presents for their children won't soon forget the knock on the door that Christmas Eve with gifts for their children from a neighbor they never met.

The waitress wondering how she would pay for her next meal, who received an unexpected hundred-dollar tip from the most unlikely customer that day, won't soon forget.

The relatives of victims at Sandy Hook and the other schools where unexpected and horrific violence took the lives of innocent children, won't forget how entire communities rallied around them, pouring out love and kindness when the violence disrupted the lives of so many people.

Who are these people who mail random checks, leave large tips, buy Christmas presents for kids in need, and rally around the victims of violence? Often, they are the people who, themselves, were the beneficiary of a kindness in their lives that so moved them, they decided to pay it forward.

One thing I have learned is don't try to pay love back, pay it forward.

> I have given you a model to follow,
> so that as I have done for you, you
> should also do. (John 13:15 NAB)

Isn't it time we all worked at paying it forward? It can be something very simple. We can donate clothing, give blood, volunteer, be a big brother, help a stranded motorist fix a flat, stop by the neighbor kid's lemonade stand. There are literally hundreds of small things we can do.

All we need to do is keep our antenna up, by being attentive to opportunities to help others, especially someone we don't know.

Think back over your life. Have there been acts of kindness that you remember, where at just the right moment God put someone in your path that you will never forget? Remember, you can't pay love back, but you can pay it forward.

You can be the person that happens by just at the right moment, the person that they will remember for a lifetime.

Reflections: *Have you ever been the recipient of a random act of kindness? Does it make you feel like "paying it forward?" Can you remember someone in your past because of their kindness?*

Girls with Purple Hair

Therefore, you are without excuse,
every one of you who passes judgment. For by the standard by which
you judge another you condemn
yourself, since you, the judge, do
the very same things. (Romans 2:1
NAB)

A few weeks ago, while Diane was in California visiting our grandsons, I was driving to get some dinner when I witnessed a traffic
accident. A woman pulling out of a gas station hit a young man on
a motorcycle.

As I approached the scene, I couldn't help but notice that cars
were swerving to avoid the driver, who lay in pain in the middle of
the street, and his bike that was now a twisted mess. No one was
stopping to help!

As I pulled my car into a nearby parking lot, a young woman with
purple hair and a funky outfit ran into the middle of the street, and
with all the strength she could muster, half-carried and half-
dragged the injured cyclist to the curb.

As I approached them, a woman informed us that she had called
911 and an ambulance was on the way.

The rider was in shock, his left hand mangled. As I tried to tend to
his wound as best I could, the girl with the purple hair consoled
him in a soft voice, talking to him and getting him to talk with her.

What I observed in the next few minutes was compassion, caring,
and empathy, from the most unlikely person. Or was she?

As the medics from EMS took over and got the injured man into the ambulance, I asked the young girl why she ran into the street to help. Her answer was simple, "Because he was in danger and was suffering, and I know and understand suffering."

The truth is I have a soft spot for girls with purple hair! I like the Goth girls, the misfits, and the loners, too. These are the high school kids that don't seem to fit in. They aren't part of the click; cheerleaders, jocks, or beauty queens. They have been ignored, made fun of, bullied, and treated badly.

Girls with purple hair, I learned, understand suffering.

If you are bleeding, lying in the middle of the street, they will be the first to help! Remember:

> The loneliest people are the kindest.
> The saddest people are the bright-
> est. The most damaged people are
> the wisest. All because they do not
> wish to see anyone else suffer the
> way they do.[1] —Tony Agnesi

Spend a little time with any social service agency, homeless shelter, hospice, woman's shelter, or food pantry, and what will you always see? Girls with purple hair!

Let's face it: we are judgmental. If you were interviewing for a new employee, would purple hair, a tattoo, or piercing turn you off? Would you be quick to dismiss the applicant? Or would you take the time to get to know them before passing judgment?

The next time you encounter a girl with purple hair; don't be so quick to judge. Take some time to get to know her, and you might be surprised by what you'll discover.

If you are ever alone, injured, in the middle of the road, she might just be the one to drag you to safety.

Reflections: Do we often judge people by their looks? Does purple hair or a tattoo affect the way you look at someone? Have you ever found the most unlikely people to be the most caring

CHAPTER THREE

God s Grace in Hard Times

Enter Into My Rest

> Forty years I loathed that genera-
> tion; I said: "This people's heart
> goes astray; they do not know my
> ways." Therefore, I swore in my
> anger: "They shall never enter my
> rest." (Psalm 95:10–11, NAB)

> Therefore, let us be on our guard
> while the promise of entering into
> his rest remains, that none of you
> seem to have failed. (Hebrews 4:1,
> NAB)

Every day, as I begin the Divine Office, the phrase, "enter into my
rest" seems to jump off the page.

What is this rest? What did the Israelites do to fail to enter into it?
More importantly, what can we do to enter into God's rest?

Ultimately, we are talking about that eternal rest with God in Heaven. Nevertheless, it was the Israelites disbelief and loss of faith in God that caused them to murmur against him and desire to go back to their slavery under the Egyptians instead of the Promised Land.

Instead, the next generation, under the leadership of Joshua, entered into the land of Canaan, into God's rest.

Disbelief, not putting their faith in God's hands, is what caused the Israelites to not enter into that rest.

What about us? Is God's rest still available to us? How do we enter into that rest?

The good news is that the promise remains! We have, and continue to receive, the good news through the Gospels, and we just need to *believe it.* We need to accept the offer and trust totally in God's promise.

Easier said than done, right?

The truth is, we either trust ourselves to save ourselves or we trust God, for our salvation through the life, death, and resurrection of his Son, Jesus Christ, on the cross. It is either one or the other!

For many of us, talking a good game isn't the same as living it. We trust in God to a point, but when the going gets tough, we tend to rely on our belief in ourselves to get us through difficult circumstances. We just can't take that final step of surrender that leads to entering into God's rest. We become like the Israelites who hear the Word, but just can't surrender totally.

So, what can we do to enter into God's rest?

1. We must realize we can't do it on our own. We need to have faith through the grace of God. As Ephesians 2:8–9 remind us, "For by grace you have been saved through faith, and this is not from you; it is the gift of God; it is not from works, so no one may boast." We need to accept this gift from God and ask for His grace.

2. We have got to believe, not just to a point but total faith in Christ and obedience to his will. Total surrender, putting outcomes in God's hands and not relying on our own devices, is the only way. Anything less and we are no better than our ancestors in the desert.

3. We must encourage each other. As Hebrews 3:13 tells us, "Encourage yourselves daily while it is still 'today,' so that none of you may grow hardened by the deceit of sin." It should be our goal not only to enter into His rest ourselves, but help our spouses, children, family, and friends overcome their disbelief. After all, we all have our own moments of disbelief.

4. We must find truth in the Gospels. We must not only receive the Good News but profit from it. As Hebrews 4:2 explains, "For in fact we have received the good news just as they did. But the word that they heard did not profit them, for they were not united in faith with those who listened."

 5. We must "Keep the faith." God's rest is available to all of us. However, we must believe, surrender ourselves to the will of God, pray for His grace, encourage others, and find Truth in the Gospels.

We all need God's rest. He offers it to us through His Son, Jesus Christ. Let's encourage each other to remain faithful in our belief, share the Gospels, and together enter into his heavenly rest.

Reflections: *We all need God's rest. How are you entering into His rest? How would you define God's rest? How does faith help us enter into God's rest?*

Making It Through Hard Times

> The God of all grace who called
> you to his eternal glory through
> Christ [Jesus] will himself restore,
> confirm, strengthen, and establish
> you after you have suffered a little.
> (1 Peter 5:10, NAB)

We are all going to have hard times. Some of us get through them better than others. You would never know what some people experience. They can maintain a positive attitude, continue to be grateful, live in the moment, and offer their sufferings up to God, by placing their troubles at the foot of the cross.

Others don't do so well. They suffer openly, have a negative, destructive attitude, and feel that their happiness has been shortchanged. They wear their pain on their shoulders for everyone to see. They make themselves miserable by obsessing over their problems.

What can help us make it?

1.   **Know that pain and suffering are part of life.** We are taught from an early age to avoid pain. Don't touch the hot stove. Look both ways before crossing the road. Be careful or you'll poke an eye out. All these lessons are drilled into us. The truth is, we will all face adversity in our lives; some more than others. An illness, job loss, relationship breakup, loss of a loved one—we are all going to experience something painful, sorrowful, or humiliating. Nevertheless, we grow through what we experience. Life's greatest lessens are learned through tough times, not pain-free times.

2.   **Attitude is everything.** When we are faced with adversity we have two choices: accept it and let go of the negativity that comes with it, or obsess over it, and in doing so become anxious and miserable.

3.   **You can't change the situation, but you can change yourself.** You will never change until you take responsibility for your attitude. It's amazing that when we change ourselves, our circumstances change too! Not the other way around.

4.   **No matter the situation, there is always some reason to be thankful.** An attitude of gratitude can help us overcome any situation. No matter what we have experienced, we still have many reasons to be thankful. There is always someone who would happily exchange places with us.

5.   **Don't compare yourself to others.** Don't rely on others to validate you. Remember, the friends that seem to be living the perfect life are having struggles of their own. Your situation may pale compared to theirs. You may never know the extent of their suffering.

6.   **You are not alone, and things will change.** I learned at a young age that, other than death and taxes, the only thing certain is that things will change. As the old saying goes, "This too shall pass!" Anything is possible, but great things often take time.

7.   **In God, all things are possible.** Do you believe that miracles can happen? I do. I've seen and read of hundreds. I've experienced them myself. You can too!

Put your troubles in God's hands. Trust that He will get you through your hard times and grant you the peace that surpasses all understanding. It's a peace that will guard your heart and mind, until He sees you through your pain.

Reflections: *How has God helped you through hard times? What are your feelings about suffering? Is there anything we can learn from experiencing hard times?*

Thirty Days to Live

Teach us to count our days aright,
that we may gain wisdom of heart.
(Psalm 90:12, NAB)

What if you only had one month to live? What would you do if the doctor said to get your affairs in order in the next 30 days? How would you live your life if you knew with certainty that your days on earth were numbered?

Would you do anything differently? Would you make some changes in the way you are currently living your life?

Would you spend more time with your kids and really listen when they talk with you?

Would you look at your spouse the same way you did when you were dating?

Would you stop to smell the roses, take in a sunset, or enjoy the sounds of nature?

Would you call an old friend that you haven't seen in years?

What about your faith?

Would you pray more, attend Mass more frequently, be grateful for little things, and be more forgiving of those that have hurt you in the past?

Important questions, right? However, we rarely ever take the time to think about these questions. We live as if there is no running clock, as if we will be on earth forever. Questions to be put off for a later time, when we are older, when old age brings us closer to the certainty of death.

Occasionally, these are questions to be dealt with now. Things like a cancer diagnosis, a bad automobile accident, or a bad fall on the ice can force us to ask these questions immediately.

I can remember vividly how my focus changed when I was diagnosed with colon cancer eight years ago. I was going about living my life with a "soft focus" filter on; everything was pleasantly moving along.

That cancer diagnosis brought everything into focus. It is a sharp, clear focus where things that I never thought about suddenly became important. Like many others before me, I began to ask these tough questions about change, about priorities, about what is really important.

I learned that our time here on earth is short. We weren't made for this life, but for the next. We were made for eternal life; for heaven.

If you are honest with yourself and ask these questions, you will make some changes. You will do things differently. You will become a better person.

As a matter of fact, you will become the most authentic version of yourself. Your spouse will notice the changes, as will your kids, your friends, and everyone around you. You will become the "you" that God intended you to be.

Last week, eight years later, I had a biopsy for possible prostate cancer. The biopsy forced me to ask these questions once again. The possibility of a new cancer made me ask the question, "What if?"

This week, I got the results. There was no cancer. I'm 100 percent cancer free! It was a scare for sure, but a bad thing? No! Occasionally, God has to take drastic actions to get our attention. I praise God and thank him for this blessing. I also thank the many people who kept me in their prayers these past few weeks.

The next chance you get, take some time to ask yourself, *what if I had only 30 days to live?* Then, have the courage to make the changes necessary to become the most authentic "you" that you can be. It's the "you" God intended.

Reflections: Have you ever had a life-changing experience that changed the way you think about death? What would you do differently if you only had one month to live? Are you living as the most authentic version of yourself?

Wonderfully Flawed

But we hold this treasure in earthen vessels, that the surpassing power may be of God and not from us. We are afflicted in every way, but not constrained; perplexed, but not driven to despair; persecuted, but not abandoned; struck down, but not destroyed; always carrying about in the body the dying of Jesus, so that the life of Jesus may also be manifested in our body. (2 Corinthians 4:7–10, NAB)

I praise you, so wonderfully you made me; wonderful are your works! My very self you knew. (Psalm 139:14, NAB)

A child is born, and we look in the bassinet and say, "She is perfect!" Ten fingers and ten toes, seven pounds of pure joy, wonderfully made through the miracle of life.

We use the term "perfect" even though we all understand that we are human. We are not perfect. We all are flawed in some way.

For some people, flaws can be obvious, such as being born blind or deaf, with a deformed hand, cleft pallet, or clubbed foot.

For others, the flaws aren't visible. We look perfect, but we suffer from a mental illness: depression, bi-polar disorder, attention deficit disorder or autism.

For some, an accident can damage us, both physically and mentally. A soldier that loses a leg stepping on a land mine in the field of battle, a child burned from an accident, or a highway crash that causes the victim to be confined to a wheel chair, can alter life forever.

For still others, small things may be perceived as flaws. We may feel we are too fat or too thin, too tall or too short, our hair is too straight or too curly, or our ears too big.

No matter how big or small these flaws are, many people feel as though they have been dealt the wrong cards. They wish God had dealt them a "better hand."

However, if we believe that God doesn't make junk, that we are all wonderfully made, we also must accept that everything that God gives us is for a reason. We are all a work in progress, we are all wonderfully flawed. We are "earthen vessels" made of clay and molded by the hands of God.

What we do with these flaws says a lot about our faith. Some people just can't handle the flaws. Yet others, in spite of their flaws, use them for the glory of God.

The soldier whose legs were amputated motivates others with his performance on Dancing with the Stars. As he overcomes his flaws and gives hope—he is wonderfully flawed.

The burn victim that visits the local children's hospital to let younger victims know they aren't alone—she is wonderfully flawed.

The successful blind businessman who volunteers to teach braille to others offers himself as a role model for success—he is wonderfully flawed.

The parents of a child born with a cranial deformity who write and speak, and form support groups, are giving hope to other parents facing the same issues—because their beautiful child is wonderfully flawed.

The college basketball player who plays through her cancer diagnosis and squeezes every second out of a life cut too short, inspires others and leaves a legacy—she is wonderfully flawed.

You see, we all have flaws and we all have the ability to take the hand we are dealt and play it for the glory of God. We can be a blessing to others. We can turn our weaknesses into strengths. We can make a difference, wonderful flaws and all.

The next time you are feeling sorry for yourself, remember that others have been given a much more difficult life. The person that you think has the perfect life has problems that we can't even imagine. Let's take our flaws and turn them into a blessing.

Each of us can take our personal crosses and unite them with the cross of our Savior, longing for the perfection that we will have in heaven. But, for now, understand that we are all wonderfully flawed.

Reflections: *Do you sometimes feel that you have been dealt a bad hand? What are your flaws? Do you ever allow your flaws to define you?*

Let's Practice Humility

When he is dealing with the arrogant, he is stern, but to the humble he shows kindness. (Proverb 3:34, NAB)

Whoever exalts himself will be humbled; but whoever humbles himself will be exalted. (Matthew 23:12, NAB)

Likewise, you younger members, be subject to the presbyters. And all of you, clothe yourselves with humility

in your dealings with one another,
for: "God opposes the proud but
bestows favor on the humble." (1
Peter 5:5, NAB)

There is something about humility that I find very appealing. I love
to see a quarterback thank his linemen for the great blocking following the big game.

Or when a passerby who saves a child from a burning house is
called a hero and his response is, "No, I'm not a hero; anyone
would have done the same thing."

Or when a businessperson or athlete who is presented with an
award shares the moment with his fellow teammates, thanking
them by name.

I get excited when they realize that their talents and ability are a
gift from God, and they give Him thanks. Mother Teresa has said
that "humility is the mother of all virtues."[1] Yes, I think we are all
attracted to humility!

Nobody likes arrogance and cockiness. Braggarts turn us off. Unfortunately, something is happening in our society today. Today's
society thinks humility is an old-fashioned virtue. Today's athletes
are thumping their chests with a "look at me" narcissistic strut.
Society has no place for humility. It's all about *me first*!

I read that a few years ago Google released a database of over five
million books. In it, the use of the words "kindness" and "happiness" dropped 56% between 1960 and 2008. Meanwhile, the
words "modesty" and "humility" dropped 52%. It's no wonder we
live in an unkind and angry world where modesty and humility are
considered weaknesses.

Somehow, we have a misunderstanding of humility. Maybe understanding what it *is not* will help. Humility is not allowing people to
push you around. It's not avoiding conflict or hiding your feelings.
It certainly isn't about being a doormat or playing the victim or
martyr.

Humility is about giving credit and respect where it is due, remaining faithful to our promises, refraining from despair, and confronting our fears and uncertainty. Rather than glorifying ourselves, it means giving glory to God, for the talents and ability He has given us.

A wonderful thing happens when we practice humility. It liberates us from society's "me first" narcissism. It stops the constant comparison to others.

We understand and appreciate that we are all given different gifts and that in recognizing someone's talent and ability; we don't diminish those gifts that God gave us.

When we give credit and respect to others, recognizing their talent and ability, it elevates people's opinions about us. People genuinely love humble people!

In her book, *The Joy in Loving: A Guide to Daily Living,*[2] Saint Mother Teresa gives a list of a few ways we can practice humility:

- o   To speak as little as possible of one's self.

- o   To mind one's own business.

- o   Not to want to manage other people's affairs.

- o   To avoid curiosity.

- o   To accept contradictions and correction cheerfully.

- o   To pass over the mistakes of others.

- o   To accept insults and injuries.

- o   To accept being slighted, forgotten, and disliked.

- o   To be kind and gentle even under provocation.

- o   Never to stand on one's dignity.

- o   To choose always the hardest.

And if Mother Teresa's suggestion for practicing humility doesn't suit your fancy, consider the *Litany of Humility* prayer. I added it to my daily prayers for a number of months and still pray it frequently. It was difficult at first; the words just not resonating well with me. But, as I prayed it, I found myself thinking of others first, asking them how their lives were going, praising them for their accomplishments and letting them know how proud I was of the person they were becoming. As I did, happiness followed.

Give it a try every day for just one week. See if it makes a difference in your life. See if being liberated from society's "Me First" narcissism is a step toward a happier life.

Prayer: The Litany of Humility

O Jesus! meek and humble of heart, **Hear me.**
From the desire of being esteemed,
Deliver me, Jesus.

From the desire of being loved…
From the desire of being extolled …
From the desire of being honored …
From the desire of being praised …
From the desire of being preferred to others…
From the desire of being consulted …
From the desire of being approved …
From the fear of being humiliated …
From the fear of being despised…
From the fear of suffering rebukes …
From the fear of being calumniated …
From the fear of being forgotten …
From the fear of being ridiculed …
From the fear of being wronged …
From the fear of being suspected …

That others may be loved more than I,
Jesus, grant me the grace to desire it.

That others may be esteemed more than I …
That, in the opinion of the world,
others may increase and I may decrease …
That others may be chosen and I set aside …
That others may be praised and I unnoticed …
That others may be preferred to me in everything…
That others may become holier than I, provided that I may be-
come as holy as I should…[3]

Reflections: *How well do you follow Mother Teresa's list of ways to be humbler? Have you ever prayed the Litany of Humility? Is being liberated from society's "Me First" narcissism a step toward a happier life?*

Overcoming Disappointment

I will never forsake you or abandon you. (Hebrews 13:5, NAB)

Rejoice in hope, endure in affliction, and persevere in prayer.
(Romans 12:12, NAB)

In all circumstances give thanks, for this is the will of God for you in Christ Jesus. (1 Thessalonians 5:18, NAB)

We know that all things work for good for those who love God, who are called according to his purpose. (Romans 8:28, NAB)

Let's face it. There is no way around it. We will all experience dis-
appointment. It is a natural and normal part of life. We have high expectations for ourselves and others, but often, we don't live up to those expectations.

Jennifer was disappointed that she didn't get the job that she thought was a perfect fit for her skills. She was disappointed in herself, the company, and the process. Her disappointment turned into discouragement.

Bill was disappointed that after the undefeated season his baseball team enjoyed, they lost in the finals to a team they should have beaten. Bill was disappointed in himself, his teammates, and coaches. He questioned whether he should return next season.

Sue thought she and Tom had the perfect marriage, until the day Tom announced he was leaving her and the kids because he had fallen in love with his secretary. Sue's disappointment turned quickly to depression and desperation.

Brian anxiously awaited the test results from his surgery. He was devastated when the surgeon told him that the cancer was worse than they expected. He was disappointed with the doctor, as well as discouraged and angry with God.

Yes, we will all experience disappointment.

So, what can we do when we experience disappointment? How do we keep from becoming discouraged or depressed?

Here are some thoughts:

1. **Take some time to grieve**. Often disappointments are devastating. They require time to heal, to reflect, and to try to understand. Know, however, as St. Paul tells us in Romans, "We know that all things work for good for those who love God, who are called according to his purpose" (8:28, NAB).

2. **Examine your perspective and expectations.** We have high expectations for others. Often, people won't live up to our vision of them. This is especially true for family members. We sometimes have unrealistic expectations for our children, spouses, and parents. It has been said that when you have high expectations, you are setting yourself

up for disappointment. Put your expectations into proper perspective.

3. **Turn toward, and not away from, God.** When people are discouraged they often make the mistake of blaming God, of going into a shell, no longer attending church, and they stop praying. These are times when we should turn toward our Lord; to gain strength from His promise to us, that He is with us always; that He will never abandon us; that He will see us through the problem and gives us a way out.

4. **Focus on hope.** We need to put our faith in God that he will give us a reason to hope. If we dwell on our Lord and not on the disappointment, we will begin to see that there is a light at the end of the tunnel. That light begins with our hope.

5. **Be grateful for the good things in our lives.** Often, we spend so much time on our problems and disappointments that we fail to take a look at the blessings. We may have lost out on that job, but there will be other opportunities and we still have the God-given skills. We may be disappointed at losing the big game, but we still have a season full of good memories to motivate us next year.

> In all circumstances give thanks, for this is the will of God for you in Christ Jesus. (1 Thessalonians 5:18, NAB)

We all face disappointments during our lives. Dealing with disappointments, by trusting in God and His promises, will go a long way to improving mental health and happiness.

Reflections: *What can we do when we experience disappointment? Do you have a method of coping with disappointment that works for you? Do you ever find yourself blaming God for your disappointments?*

Someone Touched Me

But Jesus said, "Someone has
touched me; for I know that power
has gone out from me." When the
woman realized that she had not
escaped notice, she came forward
trembling. Falling down before
him, she explained in the presence
of all the people why she had
touched him and how she had been
healed immediately. He said to her,
"Daughter, your faith has saved
you; go in peace." (Luke 8:46–48,
NAB)

"So, also, faith of itself, if it does
not have works, is dead." (James
2:17, NAB)

In the gospel of Luke, we read of a woman who had been hemor-
rhaging for twelve years. She spent everything she had to find a
cure, but to no avail. As Jesus walked through a crowd of people,
she came up behind him and touched the tassel of his cloak. Immediately, her bleeding stopped, and she was cured.

At that time in history, it was unlawful for a woman to touch any
man or his clothing. Furthermore, by virtue of her bleeding, she
would have been declared unclean and would not have been allowed to be in a crowd of people. In essence, she broke the law!
But Jesus said, "Someone has touched me; for I know that power
has gone out from me." (Luke 8:46, NAB)

As the crowd grew, many people were pushing on Jesus and his
apostles. But this was different. It wasn't accidental contact. This
woman made a point of touching the cloak of Jesus on purpose!

When she realized that Jesus was aware of her contact, she humbly
came forward and explained why she had touched him and that

she was immediately healed. Jesus's reaction surprised the crowd. He said, "Daughter, your faith has saved you; go in peace." (Luke 8:48, NAB)

Two things are significant here. One is that she approached Jesus ashamed and humble. As she reached out to touch his cloak, she was cured, not by any magical powers of his garment, but by her faith in Him.

And second, Jesus, recognizing this faith, asked her to profess it verbally before all. In fear and trembling, she explained to everyone what had happened.

When she finished, Jesus called her "daughter," a phrase he used very sparingly in the Gospels and assured her that her faith had saved her.

Do we share the same faith as the woman in this parable? Are we willing to put our faith in Jesus, even if we have exhausted all other means? When we receive healing from our Lord, are we willing to humbly share our story with others?

Are we willing to say, "I believed, I touched, I was healed?"

Not only was it a quiet faith that saved her, but also her willingness to declare that faith; to put her faith into action, for which our Lord offered her peace.

Isn't that what we all want? We know that we will, at some time in our lives, have suffering and troubles. But to have peace in the midst of these troubles makes things bearable.

Jesus has compassion for the marginalized, the unclean, women, foreigners, and even the thief crucified next to Him on the cross. Jesus will not hold himself apart from them; but is fully present in His compassion.

He has that same compassion for you!

Are you facing an illness that has you stressed out? Believe, touch, and be healed.

Is your marriage on the rocks? Believe, touch, and be healed.

Have you recently lost your job and find it tough to find a new one? Believe, touch, and be healed.

Have your adult children left the faith and nothing you can say will bring them back to God? Believe, touch, and be healed.

We need to put our complete trust in Jesus. We need to touch Him with our prayers and adoration. We will be healed by His compassion.

He will call you daughter, or son, and grant you his precious gift of peace.

Reflections: *In times of need, do you put your trust in Jesus? Do you have a story where you have said I believed, I touched, and I was healed? Do you share the same faith as the woman in the parable?*

The Heroin Epidemic; a Christian Response

> No trial has come to you but what is human. God is faithful and will not let you be tried beyond your strength; but with the trial he will also provide a way out, so that you may be able to bear it. (1 Corinthians 10:13, NAB)

Years ago, heroin addicts were portrayed as bums lying in gutters shooting up, barely alive. Heroin was a scary drug. I couldn't imagine myself, or any of my friends, ever using it. All that has changed!

In case you haven't been listening, we have a heroin epidemic in America. The people most affected are members of your own family; average middle-class kids and young adults.

They are from good families, with caring and loving parents. They are the young man, or woman, next door.

This week, our jail ministry team talked to twenty-seven men and women during our services at the local county jail. Most were between 18 and 34 years old. **All** but two were addicted to heroin. They looked nothing like the images from the past. They looked like anyone you would see at the local shopping mall or grocery store.

Talking with them, we saw the direct correlation between heroin use and the use and abuse of prescription drugs. Forty-five percent of heroin users began with pain killers like Percocet and OxyContin, according to the Center for Disease Control. And most used other drugs like cocaine, marijuana, and alcohol too.

A 35-year-old construction worker hurts his back in a job-related accident. His doctor prescribes Oxycodone, which provides relief so that he can continue to do his job and support his family. When the prescription expires, the back-pain returns. The pain prevents him from going to work. Oxy is expensive on the street. Heroin isn't. A few weeks later, he is snorting heroin and working again. Later, he begins injecting it.

A freshman basketball player is offered a prescription pain killer by a senior on the team. He says, "Try this and you will play better." Three years later, in his senior year, he begins shooting heroin. Two years later, he is in jail.

Another young man's addiction was so strong that he stole money from his mother's purse on Mother's Day and sold his 2-year-old son's Christmas presents to buy the drug. His best friend died from an overdose just a few weeks earlier, and another friend had just been arrested.

The women we talked to shared their stories of prescription drugs leading to heroin, as well.

Arresting and imprisoning addicts doesn't address the crisis. We need prevention, treatment, and overdose reduction with the help of naloxone.

So, what should our response be to the heroin epidemic? What should we, as Catholics and Christians, be doing to help? We can no longer bury our heads in the sand and rationalize that this is someone else's problem. It is a problem we all share! If you have a family member or friend who is addicted to heroin, here are some things that you can do:

1. **Let them know that they are loved by God.** Often addicts allow their additions to define their identity. That's not who they are! They are sons and daughters of the Most High. Asking God for His help, through prayer, is a powerful way to aid the healing process.

2. **Let them know that they are not the first and are not alone.** Others have been lured into drug use, just as they have, and have sought and found recovery. They can too!

3. **Let them know that overcoming addictions are difficult and painful, and calling on a higher power helps.** The twelve-step programs of Alcoholics and Narcotics Anonymous do work. I have observed that overcoming heroin addictions alone is nearly impossible. Calling on a higher power, God, as we Christians would describe Him, is the path with the greatest success. Pray with them!

4. **Let them know, that you are here to help them.** Even if it is just someone to talk to, someone to encourage their journey to successful recovery, someone to drive them to a meeting, recovery group, or to pray with them, you can be a blessing.

5. **Let them know that you are not judging them by their addiction.** Yes, they have made a mistake and drug abuse

is sinful, but we must love the sinner and hate the sin. Extend to them love and forgiveness and keep them in your prayers.

6. **Let them know, that you will support the efforts to find a solution to this epidemic.** The more we know about the heroin epidemic and the more we get involved with our votes and our financial support for rehabilitation facilities and programs, the quicker we can stem the tide of overdose deaths from this horrible drug.

As Christians, let's try to be part of the solution. Our own families, friends, and neighbors' lives are in the balance.

Reflections: *What can we do to address this epidemic? As Christians, do we have a responsibility to do whatever we can? Would you support a heroin clinic in your town or neighborhood?*

Father's Day Without Dad

> As you know, we treated each one of you as a father treats his children, exhorting and encouraging you and insisting that you conduct yourselves as worthy of the God who calls you into his kingdom and glory. — (1 Thessalonians 2:11–12, NAB)

> As a father has compassion on his children, so the LORD has compassion on the faithful. (Psalm 103:13, NAB)

Today is Father's Day, the one day each year that we honor Dad. Fatherhood is one of the most important roles in life and one that

I have always taken seriously. Being a dad, mentor at the jail, coach, uncle, and grandpa are the most meaningful roles I have ever performed. Yes, I love being a father!

But on Father's Day, it is important to note that one in three kids today grows up without a father. Single moms have become more commonplace and the lack of influence of a father figure in a child's life is one of the main causes in the breakdown of family life. Some men today just don't understand the importance of being present for their kids.

Others, through no fault of their own, have lost their fathers. Accidents and illnesses have claimed decent men, wonderful fathers, and terrific teachers too soon. For some lucky kids, an uncle, neighbor, grandfather or family friend will fill that role. These unofficial dads are special people. They become the surrogate father figures that will never be forgotten.

My friend Bob lost his dad at age 3. The men in the neighborhood rose to the occasion and many became unofficial dads. Recently, he shared:

"I was lucky, in a way, because every father in my neighborhood became my father in my mind. If I did something wrong or something good, one of them would say so. I felt lucky and thanked them later in my life when I saw them."

Father's Day reminds all of us just how much we miss our fathers. I often wish that my Dad was around to share in my success, to get to know his great grandsons, or to just enjoy a fishing trip, round of golf, or a great meal together. So, I have adopted a few older friends as unofficial fathers and have enjoyed times with them in his honor.

Many of you reading this might be experiencing their first Father's Day without Dad. The first year following the death of a father is a tough one. Christmas, his birthday, Easter, and annual family gatherings become sad times that were once happy ones. Father's Day is one of those. I understand.

What can we do to make that day a memorable one and less difficult? Here are a few things to try:

1. **Do something he enjoyed**. A cookout, ballgame, or family gatherings are a great way to keep his memory alive.

2. **Tell a story**. Even though Dad is not there, share stories, lessons he taught you, and funny things he said over the years that made you laugh.

3. **Honor him with your fatherhood**. The best way to honor your father is with your own fatherhood. Let your kids see how much you love their mother. And if you don't have your own kids, become an unofficial dad to a kid, or kids, in need.

4. **Do things that would have made him proud**. Work hard, be kind and generous, make your family a priority and be a father figure to those who have no father.

5. **Don't forget your heavenly Father**. Saint Joseph has always been one of my favorite saints. We don't know much about him from the Bible, but we do know he shared the same title with God. That title was "Father." To Jesus, Joseph was his earthly father and God his heavenly father! God is your heavenly father too!

How will you celebrate Dad today? How can you honor him with your own fatherhood? Happy Father's Day!

Reflections: *Jesus called His Father "Abba." What do you call your father? Do you have a good relationship with your father?*

The Quest for Rest

Come to me, all you who labor and
are burdened, and I will give
you rest. Take my yoke upon you
and learn from me, for I am meek
and humble of heart; and you will
find rest for yourselves. For my
yoke is easy, and my burden light.
(Matthew 11:28–30, NAB)

On the seventh day God was finished with the work he had been
doing; he rested on the seventh day
from all the work he had undertak-
en. So God blessed the seventh day
and made it holy, because on it he
rested from all the work he had
done in creation. (Genesis 2:2–3,
NAB)

Return, my soul, to your rest; the
LORD has been very good to you.
(Psalm 116:7, NAB)

Do you ever feel guilty when you take some time to rest? Has society somehow convinced you that rest is an indulgence you simply
can't afford? In this go-go society of never ending to-do lists and
late-night text messages from work, we are obsessed with the feeling that we should constantly be doing something!

Add to that stress the expectations of the new job, new house, and
new baby who wakes every night at 4 a.m., and we just can't find
the time to give ourselves a break.

Rest is important! Scientific studies prove that getting the proper
amount of rest and relaxation has valuable health benefits. Rest
protects our heart, lowers the risk of stroke, boosts our memory,

and improves our decision making. Rest helps prevent colds, reduces acne, helps keep us slim, and helps fight breast cancer.

So, why do we feel guilty when we take a break? Why do we feel that we have to be busy all the time?

The Bible speaks often of rest. At least 72 times, the Bible tells us of the importance of rest. Even God rested on the seventh day!

I remember fondly the Sundays of my youth. My family's day began with Mass, and then we spent the remainder of the day with family: Mom and Dad, aunts and uncles, grandma and grandpa, and all the kids. We just spent time doing nothing, just enjoying each other's company, and entering into that Sabbath rest.

It was easier then. Businesses were closed on Sunday. There was no mall, no Sunday liquor sales, and no after-hours messages from work. Just relaxation!

Everything has changed. Stores are open, people are working, business emails are flowing, and people are glued to their smart phones for fear that they might miss an important text message.

So, let me share some good news: it doesn't have to be that way!

That's right. You have the power to decide to disconnect and enter into that sweet rest. All those challenges, emails, and text messages with still be there tomorrow.

Here are a few ideas on how to make rest and relaxation part of your life:

1. **Take a break**. Studies have shown that taking a 15-minute break after every hour we work increases our productivity. In my own experience, I like to work hard on a task for one hour, then take a break. I walk around, grab a bottle of water, step outside and breathe some fresh air, or have a brief conversation with an associate. I then return to my office refreshed and ready to tackle another task.

2. **Make time for downtime.** When you are creating that to-do list, make sure you schedule some down time. That's right; it is just as important as anything else on the list. Walk to lunch, take a jog, pray, meditate, or take a nap—remember, schedule these breaks!

3. **Make rest part of your routine.** Find something at the beginning and end of each day to help you relax. For me, praying the Chaplet of Divine Mercy in my car on the way to work makes for a more mindful day. Shutting off smart phones, computers, television, and other devices an hour before bedtime helps the process of relaxation.

4. **Get at least 7 hours of sleep.** Although difficult when your little one wakes up twice during the night, taking turns getting up will allow at least one of you to get some needed sleep. For the rest of us, going to bed a little earlier might be the answer. If you record that 10 p.m. TV program and watch it the next day, you will get you extra sleep time.

5. **Make Sunday a true day of rest.** You probably can't do it every Sunday, but I promise that if you try it, you'll crave it every week. Start with going to church as a family. Then for the rest of the day, enjoy doing something fun together. Watch a movie, go to a ball game, the zoo, visit an amusement park, or just play board games, but do it together as a family.

Why not give these suggestions a try, or come up with your own list?

As for me, it's time for a nap!

Reflections: *What do you do to ensure you get some rest? Do you ever feel guilty for downtime? Are you getting enough sleep?*

A Lesson and a Cure

If someone who has worldly means
sees a brother in need and refuses
him compassion, how can the love
of God remain in him? Children, let
us love, not in word or speech but
in deed and truth. (1 John 3:17,
NAB)

Give thanks to the LORD, who is
good, whose love endures forever.
(Psalm 118:1, NAB)

Do not withhold any goods from
the owner when it is in your power
to act. Say not to your neighbor,
"Go, come back tomorrow, and I
will give it to you," when all the
while you have it. (Proverbs 3:27–
28, NAB)

It was the shortest doctor's appointment I ever had, but one in
which I had been waiting and praying for, for almost a decade. The
doctor walked into the room, leaned against the counter and said,
"You're cured!"

A year following my cancer surgery in a routine blood test, my
family doctor found some elevated liver enzyme levels that required some additional testing. The results were, "You have
Hepatitis C!"

Hep C, long associated with drug users, blood transfusions, and
outdated blood testing was now a reality. Did I get it from the surgery, or was this something that I had for a long time? Was it a
nick at the barber shop with an unclean razor, or intermingling

blood during a childhood reenactment of Tonto and the Lone Ranger becoming blood brothers? I'll never know.

Following the diagnosis, I discovered that the cure rate for my genotype was less than 30 percent and the treatment was a year of weekly injections and a daily pill regimen. Along with my doctor, I decided to forgo the treatment and wait for research to develop a new drug that might have a better chance of success.

Eight years later, new drugs entered the market, one of them being Harvoni. Unlike the old protocol, Harvoni involved taking one pill a day, every day, for twelve weeks. Its success rate was nearly 100 percent in my genotype.

These drugs are expensive, over $1,000 a day; $90,000 total for the twelve weeks. After three failed attempts to get insurance to cover it, I was finally approved for the treatment. I began treatment in January and completed the regimen twelve weeks later. After a month, blood work showed no signs of Hepatitis C and it was still gone after twelve additional weeks!

The protocol calls for additional blood work after three months. If the virus was still undetectable in the blood, after three months, then I would be considered cured. Yesterday, I received that news. Praise God!

As I fought back tears leaving the hospital following this wonderful news, I remembered an encounter I had just twenty hours earlier.

As I returned to work following lunch, I saw a man sitting on the ground, leaning against the wall of the building. while crying. He appeared to be in his mid-30's, disheveled, and in distress.

"Are you alright?" I questioned.

"No," was his response. "I have a prescription that I need to fill, but I don't have enough money to get it. Without these drugs, I don't know what might happen."

"Do you have the prescription with you?" I questioned.

"Yes, right here," he quickly responded.

I reached out my hand and said, "Come, right now and let's go inside and get this filled."

As we left the drug store, he hugged me, and thanked me over and over. The prescription cost less than $20.

Quite the contrast; my $90,000 treatment was made available because I have a job, a good health insurance policy, and access to the best doctors and treatment. This person, whose life was in danger for the lack of $20, had no way of meeting his own needs.

Just twenty hours before being told of my cure, God taught me a lesson in gratitude, humility, and mercy. He taught me that the best way to celebrate my blessing was to work to ensure that those same blessings are made available to the less fortunate; whether it's paying for a $20 prescription or making my voice heard in the marketplace of public opinion.

In my lifetime, God has given me two miracles: "You're cancer free!" and "You're hepatitis is cured!" I am humbled and grateful for God's mercy. If I can ask one more thing in prayer, please Lord, make the next miracle one for him.

Thank you, Lord, for the lesson and the cures!

Reflections: *Do you ever take for granted the blessings you received? With great insurance, Tony received world class care, but what about those less fortunate? Don't they deserve the same care?*

Three of Me

The one who calls you is faithful,
and he will also accomplish it. (1
Thessalonians 5:24, NAB)

If anyone wishes to come after me,
he must deny himself and take up
his cross daily and follow me. (Luke
9:23, NAB)

We all have three versions of ourselves playing in our minds. The me I was, the me I am, and the me I want to be.

We can look back into the past and remember our younger selves. Sometimes that can be a pleasant thought of a playful kid riding a bike, swimming, or playing baseball. Or, it could be a troubled child from a struggling single-parent home, being bullied, experimenting with drugs, or hanging out with a gang.

We can think about the person we are now. We might be a successful spouse and parent with a great job, beautiful home, and wonderful family and friends. Or, we might be a helpless addict, hooked on heroin because of abusing pain killers, near divorce, bankruptcy, estranged from family and friends.

We can also think about the person we truly want to be, but in doing so, we must consider the changes we need to make in our lives to get there. For some, we are already on that path. For others, it will require sacrifice, hard work, and determination to get there.

As we reflect, there are a few things we need to remember. First, the past is the past. We must put it behind us, learn from it, and refuse to dwell in it.

There is an old saying that we should exhale the past and inhale the future.

At the jail this week, we talked about releasing the past. I shared that no matter how hard or painful the past is, we can always begin again. We are never defined by our past, we just learn from it. That is the beauty of our Christian faith.

Jesus died for our sins. He died for all of us and for every sin. He offers us a new beginning, if we choose to take it—a beginning of forgiveness, redemption, and salvation. He offers us everlasting life!

But to have a future and be the person we want to be, we need to be focused on the present, live in the present, and not let yesterday take up too much of today.

How can we do this? How can we stay focused on what we need to do today to embrace our future, to be the person we want to be?

Here are a few thoughts:

1. Life happens in the present. We need to stay focused on the solutions and not focus on our troubles. We waste our time dwelling in the past.
2. We need to stay focused on Jesus. In Hebrews 2:12 we read that we should *"keep our eyes fixed on Jesus, the leader and perfecter of faith."* Jesus is always faithful to us and He is there to help us accomplish our goals.
3. We need to ask for God's help every day. A morning prayer I share with the inmates is simply this: "Jesus, help me get through this day to become the person I want to be."
4. We need to avoid distractions. Bad relationships, problems at work, traffic jams, and disappointments with others can take our focus off our goals. As we learn in Colossians 3:2, *"Think of what is above, not of what is on earth."*
5. We need to pray. Having a strong prayer life and praying every day can become a great habit. It keeps us from dwelling in the past and helps us to focus on our future, by living our best life in the present.

Yes, we all have three "me" needs. Release the "me" I was, stay focused on the "me" I am, and continue moving toward the "me" I want to be. Let's stay focused on, and be faithful to, Jesus!

Reflections: *How are you handling the transition to the "me" you are meant to be? How do you let go of the past and live in the moment? Are you having trouble putting the past behind you?*

Bitter or Better

> See to it that no one be deprived
> of the grace of God, that no bitter
> root spring up and cause trouble,
> through which many may become
> defiled. (Hebrews 12:15, NAB)

At some time in our lives, we will all face bitterness. The death of a loved one, a divorce, sickness, job loss, or a betrayal can rock your very being and send you into a pit of bitterness, self-pity, and defeat.

For many, the feelings are just temporary, but for some people, bitterness can overwhelm them and become a part of their lives, something that they can't rid. They talk about it all day, and it becomes the central focus of their lives.

They just never seem to get better.

We all know people like this. They can't get over their divorce, the loss of a child, a financial setback, losing a job, or their home. It is all they think, talk, and worry about, and they blame God!

How about you?

Have you been going through life bitter and angry? Have events of the past clouded your hope for a bright future? Do you find it difficult to even get up in the morning?

> Hatred stirs up disputes, but love covers all offenses. (Proverbs 10:12, NAB)

Do you wake up to "Good God, it's morning" instead of "Good morning, God"?

Then, you need to make the decision to get better, not bitter!

As Christians, we are not promised a pain-free life. Bad things happen to good people. Fortunately, God offers us hope and a way out.

There is an old saying: "God didn't promise days without pain, laughter without sorrow, or sun without rain, but He did promise strength for the day, comfort for the tears, and light for the way. If God brings you to it, He will bring you through it."

If we turn to Him!

In Isaiah 41:10, God offers to strengthen us: "Fear not, I am with you; be not dismayed: I am your God. I will strengthen you, and help you, and uphold you with my right hand of justice."

In 2 Corinthians 1:3, God offers comfort, compassion and encouragement: "Blessed be the God and Father of our Lord Jesus Christ, the Father of compassion and God of all encouragement, who encourages us in our every affliction."

God's "word is a lamp for my feet, a light for my path," as we read in Psalm 119:105.

You can do this, my friend!

Turn to God in prayer and ask Him to grace you with wisdom to address the bitterness, provide comfort when your emotions get the best of you, and to guide you with virtue to a happier life.

It won't be easy, but it will be worth it. Decide right now to choose getting better over getting bitter.

I'll be praying for you, my friend.

Reflections: *What steps do you take to shed bitterness and get better emotionally? Have you been going through life bitter and angry? Have events of the past clouded your hope for a bright future? Do you find the bitterness makes it difficult to even get up in the morning?*

Occupational Hazards

Blessed are they who are persecuted for the sake of righteousness, for theirs is the kingdom of heaven. Blessed are you when they insult you and persecute you and utter every kind of evil against you [falsely] because of me. Rejoice and be glad, for your reward will be great in heaven. Thus they persecuted the prophets who were before you. (Matthew 5: 10–12, NAB)

Whoever believes themselves just and judges others and scorns them is corrupt and a hypocrite. Arrogance compromises every good action, empties prayer, distances us from God and others.[4] —Pope Francis

I just reviewed a survey taken on a college campus. As part of the survey, college students were asked to state their religious affiliation. Over 40 percent replied "none." We know that many of these young adults were raised as Christians. They either left the faith or are too embarrassed to admit to being Christian.

Why would college-aged students be afraid to admit that they are Christians? Maybe it is because they face the ever-growing hazards of being a Christian. Maybe they sense the feeling of persecution that Jesus spoke of in the Beatitudes.

What insults and persecutions become occupational hazards of Christianity?

1. You will be called a hypocrite. They will imply that you say one thing and do another. They will imply that you talk a good game but fall short in your actions.

2. You will be called judgmental. They will say you are quick to find fault in others but downplay your own faults. They will say that you are prideful and think poorly of others who don't share your opinions.

3. You will be called anti-gay. They will accuse you of being intolerant. You will be accused of having a contempt for gays and lesbians and condemn their lifestyle.

4. You will be called out of touch. Your friends will think that you are old-fashioned, unintelligent and anti-science.

5. You will be called too political. As a Christian, your friends will consider you a right-winged, tea party conservative. They will say that you are living in the past.

Is it any wonder why college students won't admit to being Christian? They fear persecution, ridicule, and insults. It is safer to respond "none" when asked.

How did these perceptions become prevalent today? Is there any truth to these accusations? Have some Christians caused this to happen?

What about you?

Are you guilty of a "holier than thou" attitude? Do you judge those whose opinion differs from yours? Are you intolerant of gays and lesbians?

Each of us must do our part to overcome these perceptions. Even Pope Francis warns us not to be arrogant and judge others.

So, what can we do about it?

First, we must walk our talk. We must live our faith and not say one thing and do another. We must recognize our flaws. We are sinners too!

We must seek and find the good in others. Let's not point out their faults. Instead, let's view them as God's children, capable of following Jesus.

We should show love and compassion for everyone. Remember: hate the sin, love the sinner, and act.

We need to be informed. We need not fear engaging with others on important issues, but we need to do our homework!

We should seek to find solutions, not only by giving our opinion, but also by respecting the opinions of others.

Let's help each other avoid the occupational hazards of Christianity. We do that by living a life of faith. We need to be humble and kind, judge less and love more.

Instead of knowing us by our faults, they must know we are Christians by our love! Let's each do our part.

Reflections: Do you walk the talk?

A Shame Too Great

> No trial has come to you but what is human. God is faithful and will not let you be tried beyond your strength; but with the trial he will also provide a way out, so that you may be able to bear it. (1 Corinthians 10:13, NAB)

This past month, I began my thirteenth year in jail ministry. We have seen many changes over these past twelve years. The single biggest change is the number of inmates addicted to heroin. A large percentage of the people that our ministry team sees, on weekly basis, have a substance abuse disorder.

What are the reasons many don't seek treatment? Why does arrest and incarceration happen before treatment begins?

For many, the answer is shame and guilt.

Two female inmates shared their stories this past week. Megan (not her real name) was arrested for theft. She was living in a tent in subzero weather because of shame. She could have been staying in a warm home. Her mother and daughter would welcome her. That wasn't an option because that would mean she couldn't continue her heroin use. The drug had that much power over her. She chose to live in a freezing tent to continue using heroin, because her shame was so debilitating.

Amanda (not her real name) was arrested for heroin possession. She had been sleeping in the doorway of retail stores, trying her best to block the wind. This wasn't her first arrest. The shame and guilt were crippling.

Both women were quick to point out that they "felt free" in jail. It seems odd that being in jail made them feel free. Yet, held captive by their addiction, the shame and guilt made them feel trapped with no way out. It was a personal prison, worse than jail.

During our time together, we discussed shame and guilt. If you have a family member suffering from substance abuse, consider these points:

There is no reason for the suffering person to feel shame. They have already experienced the pain of addiction. As family and friends, we are never going to shame them into treatment.

Often, shame keeps them from seeking help. Self-esteem is low, and we need to let them know that they are not their disorder. They are good people and we love them. They have a substance disorder. We can't let them define themselves by their illness.

People with substance abuse issues blame themselves. The guilt makes them feel unworthy of treatment. They consider themselves a failure. If they suffered from any other illness or disease, no one would feel unworthy of treatment. We must help them remove the blame and let them know they deserve to live a good life. They are worthy.

There is an overwhelming feeling that others are judging them. They fear the stigma of addiction will be with them the rest of their lives. This can block them from seeking help. Some of the greatest people I know are recovering from addictions to drugs or alcohol.

The heroin epidemic has touched the lives of almost everyone. We all know someone with an addiction. At breakfast the other day a gentleman approached me. He saw me on a television interview and was moved by something I said.

He choked back his emotions and quietly shared, "I have two nephews addicted to heroin. You said that you have never met a bad person in jail, only good people who have made bad choices."

"I am in awe of what many have been through," I replied. "It is not my job to judge them, only to help point the way to recovery and love them."

Isn't that what we all should be doing?

Reflections: Are you guilty of judging people because of their drug use? Do you ever let shame and blame keep you from bettering your life? Do you have a family member or friend with a heroin problem? What can you do to help them?

Lord, If You Had Been Here

Martha said to Jesus, Lord, if you
had been here, my brother would not
have died. (John 11:21, NAB)

While on vacation in Florida, I had a chance to talk with one of the neighbors, also a vacationer. We talked briefly about baseball, the beach, and getting away from the winter snow, but then the conversation became serious.

She shared with me that she had lost her son to heroin only months before. He was in his early 20's and you could immediately tell that he was the love of her life.

"I will never get over his loss," she quietly confided. "This trip is the first time I left my house since his death."

"I'm so sorry for your loss," I replied. "I know that it is something that will always be with you."

"Thank you," she blurted out, "for not telling me that I will get over this. I will never get over this! Why does God let this happen?"

Haven't we all heard that question before? Where was God in the massacres in the Middle East? Where was God in the shootings at the mall, in schools, and movie theaters? How could God let this happen?

During Lent, we heard the gospel story of the death of Jesus's dear friend Lazarus. There is an answer to this tough question to be found in John's Gospel. (11:1–44)

Both Martha and Mary confronted Jesus with that same question. When Martha went out to meet Jesus, she must have been deeply saddened by her loss. She said to Jesus, "Lord, if you had been here, my brother would not have died." (John 11: 21, NAB)

It was almost as if she was blaming Jesus.

> Jesus said to her, "Your brother will rise." Martha said to him, "I know he will rise, in the resurrection on the last day." Jesus told her, "I am the resurrection and the life; whoever believes in me, even if he dies, will live, and everyone who lives and believes in me will never die. Do you believe this?" (John 11:23–26, NAB)

Jesus is asking that same question of each of us, especially when we have suffered a loss.

Good question, right? Do we really feel that by believing in Jesus we will never die? Do we believe that death is not the end, that we shall have eternal life?

Truth is we all will die. Some at childbirth, some after a long life, but we all will die one day. We certainly can't resent that loss and blame God for that fact.

Mary too, asked this question.

> When Mary came to where Jesus
> was and saw him, she fell at his feet
> and said to him, "Lord, if you had
> been here, my brother would not
> have died." (John 11:32 NAB)

What did Jesus do? Jesus, not only divine, but fully human as well, did what we all do: Jesus wept! Jesus loved his friend Lazarus, and He loved Lazarus' sisters, Mary and Martha, as if they were his own.

Jesus was moved to tears. Jesus mourned the loss of his friend. It is OK to mourn. It is OK to cry. It is normal, natural, and expected to have a deep sense of loss.

If we honestly believe that Jesus is the Resurrection and the Life, and we truly believe we shall never die, then we understand that our relationship and bonds with Jesus are not severed at death. Death is not the end of Jesus's bond with Lazarus, and death is not the end for us either.

The scene at the tomb has much to teach us as well.

Jesus asks Lazarus to come out of the tomb. When Lazarus did, Jesus instructed his disciples to untie him and let him go.

That is what we must do when we suffer a great loss. Remember it is OK to cry, to weep and to mourn. After all, Jesus did.

We understand that we are never going to get over the loss. We believe that our loved one is still united with Jesus. We must untie our loved one, releasing the blame and guilt and let them go to Our Lord.

For those of us who remain, there is a question in the reading for us as well.

What is the tomb of your life? What has us separated from eternal life promised by Our Lord?

Is it drugs, alcohol, sex, resentment, anger, or ego?

Then, listen to the words of our Lord and take away the stone and come out of your personal tomb. Walk away from what separates you from God and walk toward Jesus, who loves you just like he loved Lazarus, Martha, and Mary.

When my conversation with my neighbor ended, she felt as if a burden had been lifted. She had suffered a great loss. She knew it was OK to cry, to weep as Jesus wept, and that the loss would always be with her. However, she also realized that she needed to untie her son and herself from the guilt, resentment, and blame, and let him go from her loving arms to the loving arms of Jesus.

Reflections: *Does the fact that Jesus wept give you consolation that even He felt the great loss of a friend? Do you need to untie a loved one and let them go free to the arms of Jesus? What is the tomb of your life that has separated you from God?*

Who are the Lepers of Today?

When Jesus came down from the mountain, great crowds followed him. And then a leper approached, did him homage, and said, "Lord, if you wish, you can make me clean." He stretched out his hand, touched him, and said, "I will do it. Be made clean." His leprosy was cleansed

> immediately. Then Jesus said to
> him, "See that you tell no one, but
> go show yourself to the priest, and
> offer the gift that Moses prescribed;
> that will be proof for them." (Mat-
> thew 8:1-4, NAB)

There is an often-told story of St. Francis of Assisi and an encounter with a leper. I've seen many different versions. The stories
might be different, but the life lesson is the same.

Francis, and most people at that time, had a fear of lepers. When
the towns people heard the bell, that lepers were required to ring
to alert others of their presence, they would often run in the opposite direction. So did Francis.

One day, Francis had an encounter with a leper and experienced a
change of heart. As Thomas of Selano wrote in his biography of
Francis, *Remembrance of the Desire of a Soul*:

> Among all the awful miseries of this world Fran-
> cis had a natural horror of lepers, and one day as
> he was riding his horse near Assisi, he met a lep-
> er on the road. He felt terrified and revolted, but
> not wanting to transgress God's command and
> break the sacrament of His word, he dismounted
> from his horse and ran to kiss him. As the leper
> stretched out his hand, expecting something, he
> received both money and a kiss. Francis immedi-
> ately mounted his horse, and although the field
> was wide open, without any obstructions, when
> he looked around, he could not see the leper an-
> ywhere.[5]

As with Luke's account of the road to Emmaus (Luke 24:13-35),
many conclude that the leper was indeed Jesus. Francis's encounter
began his ministry to lepers near Assisi. Francis learned that the
lepers, too, were children of God.

For me, the lesson is that we often shun people that are different; those that society rejects. We stay in our safe little world assuming that it's someone else's problem.

So, who are the lepers of today? Who are the voiceless, ignored and forgotten among us? Who does society reject? More importantly, what should we, as Christians, do about it?

The mentally ill, those with physical deformities, and those with intellectual disabilities are often ignored, avoided, marginalized and forgotten. **They are the lepers of today.**

We treat the homeless, the drug addicted, the unemployed, food stamp and welfare recipients with the same disdain. **They are the lepers of today.**

The unborn, as well as the elderly suffering from Alzheimer's and dementia, are voiceless as we place convenience ahead of love for these children of God. **They are the lepers of today.**

As Francis' namesake, our current Pope Francis said, we may need to get dirty. We need to take our faith to these children of God.

Every day, as I exit the freeway on my way to work, I usually encounter a homeless person panhandling for money as motorists wait for the light to change. Occasionally, when the timing is right, and I have some cash handy, I'll roll down the window and hand the homeless person money. It may be a good deed, but it never feels right.

A few weeks ago, with temperatures in the single digits, I was amazed that a young woman was begging for money. As I reached the top of the ramp, I could see that she was shivering from the freezing cold. I was moved to roll down the window.

"You are going to get frostbite!" I yelled as she approached me.

"I am so cold, as soon as I can get money for bus fare I am return-ing to the shelter," she replied. At that moment I did something I hadn't done before.

"What's your name," I inquired. "Amanda," she replied as she broke into a huge frozen smile.

"Amanda, I would be happy to drive you to the bus stop and give you bus fare." She agreed.

As we drove the few blocks to the bus stop, she warmed herself in the car. As we waited to spot the bus, Amanda shared her story.

Amanda was begging for money for her three children. She was a single mom who had lost her job, home, and husband in the span of a few months. I gave her money for bus fare and enough to help her and her kids for a few days.

As she spotted the bus and opened to door to get out of the car, she looked at me and said, "You are the first person to call me by my name in a long time. It felt good. Can I ask your name?"

"Tony," I replied.

As she closed the door she said, "Thank you, Tony. God bless you."

"God bless you and your kids too, Amanda."

This time my good deed felt right!

So, what can we do?

1. When you are tempted to turn away from a person in need, or a person that doesn't look like you, try turning towards them instead. Smile, look them in the eyes and offer a "good morning." You might be surprised at how they might light up and smile back.

2. To be truly pro-life, we must stand up for all life from conception to the grave, which includes the homeless, mentally ill, physically handicapped, and those that don't share our lifestyle, sexual orientation, or religion.

3. Don't be afraid to "get dirty" and speak up for those who are forgotten, marginalized, and ignored—those who have no voice.

Let's let Francis be our example and serve those who are treated like lepers. We can do this.

Reflections: *Do you agree that we treat certain people in the same way as the lepers were treated in the Bible? What are you doing to embrace those that are different? Do you have any friends with mental or physical challenges?*

Scars—We All Have Them

> Other times, I look at my scars and see something else: a girl who was trying to cope with something horrible that she should never have had to live through at all. My scars show pain and suffering, but they also show my will to survive. They're part of my history that'll always be there.[6] — Cheryl Rainfield

As I was shaving in front of the bathroom mirror, I couldn't help but notice the huge scar on my stomach. It reminded me that it has been 12 years since I had surgery for colon cancer. Two feet of colon removed, and I've been cancer free for over a decade, with the ugly scar to prove it.

We all have scars, some visible and some invisible. Some physical scars are hidden by clothing; some are visible and can't be covered.

When I see scars, I see stories. A scar means you have survived, and every scar tells a story.

But what about those scars we can't see? Deep emotional scars are harder to heal. The losses of a loved one, physical and verbal abuse, bullying, divorce, abandonment, job or home loss create scars too. These scars are scars of survival that make us stronger and are proof that God heals.

> Out of suffering have emerged the strongest souls; the most massive characters are seared with scars.[7]— Kahlil Gibran

There is beauty in our scars. Scars build strength, cultivate courage, deepen our compassion for others, and make us happy to be alive. Our scars help us in other ways as well.

1. **Our scars draw us closer to Jesus.** For me, my cancer surgery and survival were like a rebirth. The soft focus of life was replaced with a sharper, clearer vision and appreciation for life. My scars reordered my priorities to faith, family, friends, and serving others.
2. **Our scars remind us of the healing power of God.** In my prayer, I realized that the hurt was over, the cancer was gone, the wound was healed, and that God had humbled me with His amazing grace.
3. **Our Scars keep us from hurting others.** When we realize that everyone has scars, we become more sensitive to the people we meet. Everyone has a story to tell. The suffering and courage that some people have endured is encouragement for us and increases our sensitivity to the scars we cannot see.
4. **Our scars remind us of our purpose.** We are called to help others, and when we have suffered, we become better equipped to help others. We can turn our scars into stars and give encouragement to others that they too can survive.

Show me your hands. Do
they have scars from giving?
Show me your feet. Are they
wounded in service? Show me
your heart. Have you left a
place for divine love?[8]—
Fulton J. Sheen

Be kind to the people you meet. You never know what they have
been through. You don't know what scars they received from what
they endured.

Twelve years cancer free and I wouldn't change a thing. I am so
grateful for what I learned these past twelve years.

Yes, we all have scars—scars that make us stronger, more coura-
geous, and deepen our compassion for others. If you have no
scars, you haven't really lived. Scars make us beautiful, because
they mean that we are alive. Thank you, Lord, for healing me and
for my scars.

Reflections: *What are your scars? Did you become stronger from having
embraced your scars? Have your personal scars made you more compassionate
to others?*

That's Not Who You Are

With all vigilance guard your heart,
for in it are the sources of life.
(Proverbs 4:23, NAB)

Over 12 years ago, when I was diagnosed with colon cancer, I remember being in an outpatient waiting room, with several other people, waiting for a test to be performed.

As I sat there, a male technician came out to the waiting room and in a loud clear voice said, "The colon cancer!" He repeated himself, "which one of you is the colon cancer?"

A few seconds passed before I realized that he was referring to me. As my anger grew, I rose to my feet and said, "My name is Tony, not 'the colon cancer'!" He sheepishly apologized.

I reacted as I did because I refused to let him define who I am.

I share this story because, often in jail ministry, we meet people that others have defined.

He's not Bill; he is the heroin addict.

She's not Debbie; she is the alcoholic.

He's not Fred; he is the drunk driver.

After a while, they begin to believe it. They let what they have done define them, not who they are.

I tell them, "You are not what you did; you are more than that. You are a son or daughter of the Most High God, made in His image and likeness. You have value, you are loved, forgiven, redeemed by His blood, and have salvation through accepting Jesus and following Him."

The same holds true for all of us. Even at an early age, people like to put people into put-down silos. Fat, ugly, crazy, jerk, dumb, spaz, goofy are some of the put-down categories they use. Over time, some people will begin to believe it.

Tell a young girl that she is ugly, and no man will ever want her. She ends up with a jerk that uses, abuses, and dominates her. If she ever speaks up, he simply pours on the abuse, reminding her that if she leaves him, no man will want her. Sadly, we see many of these women in jail, with low, or sometimes no, self-esteem.

Are you letting others define you? Are you allowing a fellow worker, a so-called friend, a parent or spouse put you into one of these silos? Is your opinion of your self-worth being reinforced by their put-downs? Do you feel unworthy, stuck with your current circumstances, unable to grow? What can you do?

Here are a few places to start:

1. **Stop putting yourself down.** Stop allowing people to bring you down to their level.
2. **Make new friends who will love and respect you.** Don't let others tell you that no one will love you. You need love the most when you feel you deserve it the least. Join a church, Bible study, a library group, a gym or exercise class. I guarantee you will meet some new friends.
3. **Don't be afraid to make mistakes.** Don't let fear stop you from trying new things or reaching out to new people.
4. **Don't try to be someone you are not.** Just try to become the most authentic version of yourself that you can be.
5. **If you have a problem, have the courage to face it.** The overweight woman that successfully diets, increases her self-esteem along with "relishing" the weight loss. The drug addict who quits not only lives a longer, healthier life, but feels compelled to help others stop as well. And with each person they help, their self-esteem rises. Rather than concentrating on perfection, focus on the progress you are making, every day, one day at a time.

6. **Stop thinking that you are not worthy of happiness.**
   Remember that you are a child of God.

You are beautiful, intelligent, and worthy. So, start believing it. Yes, there is work to do. None of us are perfect. However, we can work at becoming the most authentic version of ourselves we can be; the person God intended us to be.

Let's get to work!

Reflections: *Have you been guilty of putting yourself down? Have you ever allowed someone else to define you? Do you ever feel unworthy of happiness?*

Married and Lonely

> He said in reply, "Have you not read that from the beginning the Creator 'made them male and female' and said, 'For this reason a man shall leave his father and mother and be joined to his wife, and the two shall become one flesh'? So, they are no longer two, but one flesh. Therefore, what God has joined together, no human being must separate." (Matthew 19:4–6, NAB)

"And the two become one flesh." Wow! Marriage, as it was intended, is a beautiful thing. It is the union of man and woman that is truly the closest illustration of Christ and his Church.

There is a unity between husbands and wives: a spiritual, emotional, psychological, and financial unity. It's that "bone of my bones" oneness that we celebrate every time a bride walks down the aisle.

So, why is it that so many married people feel alone and lonely? They feel like they are living together, separately. No love, no kisses, no sex, no communication. Rather than oneness, they feel like ships crossing in the night. What happened?

Why do some couples, and even whole families, feel like they are simply living together under the same roof, but completely alone, fending for their spiritual and emotional needs by themselves?

What can we do to change this? What measures can we take to keep the fires of unity in marriage burning? Is our self-centered secular culture changing the "being one" with one another to being totally immersed in "being one" with oneself?

Here are some thoughts and ideas to increase the oneness in your marriage:

1. Put Christ at the center of your marriage. I can honestly say that having a Christ-centered marriage has contributed to the quality of my relationship with Diane. As we grow closer to Christ, we become more loving and grow closer to each other.
2. Attend Mass and pray together. When he goes early to hit the golf course and she goes later with the kids, then the oneness of family is hard to achieve.
3. Encourage your spouse's passions. Encourage her to get that degree, learn a new skill, or take that class. Encourage him to get that promotion, start a new venture, or take up a new hobby. Become a cheerleader for each other.
4. No matter how many years have gone by or how many children or grandchildren you have, continue to date each other. That's right, have a date night! Not just occasionally. Do it regularly and often.
5. Practice selfless giving. Do something to help—clearing the table after dinner, straightening up the family room after the football game, or finishing that project you have been promising to do in a timely manner. Give up something you would rather do to be with her and share, together, what she wants to do.

6. Always have a kind word, a genuine compliment, a good-bye kiss, or a loving hug. And be generous with your time.
7. Marriage is work, so work at it! We have to practice being unselfish, putting our spouses wishes ahead of our own. It is hard to be your spouse's best friend if you would rather be somewhere else with someone else.

I'm sure this isn't everything we can do, but it is a start. There are many other things we can do, as well, to keep the unity in our marriage.

Let's work together to change "married and lonely" to "married and loving it"!

Reflections: What measures have you taken to keep the fires of unity in your marriage burning? Is Christ at the center of your marriage? Do you pray together?

CHAPTER FOUR

God's Grace in the Virtues

Beautiful People Don't Just Happen

The most beautiful people we have known are those who have known defeat, known suffering, known struggle, known loss, and have found their way out of the depths. These persons have an appreciation, sensitivity, and an understanding of life that fills them with compassion, gentleness, and a deep loving concern. Beautiful people do not just happen.[1]— Elisabeth Kübler-Ross

134 · TONY AGNESI

When we think of beautiful people, we generally think of physical beauty—a beautiful young girl, a smiling baby, a handsome, athletic man. Beauty, as defined by Hollywood, the cosmetics companies, and clothing lines, are now the norm. Their image is what most people describe as beautiful.

Nevertheless, some of the most beautiful people I ever met have a different kind of beauty—a beauty that comes from loss, failure, sadness, from being to hell and back. They understand life and its hardships that tempered them and gave them an appreciation and understanding of life that increases their beauty from within.

These are the people who smile even when they face difficulties. These are the people who always have a kind word of encouragement for everyone they meet.

We often mistakenly misjudge these people. They seem to be too happy, smile too much, and have too many kind words.

We think, "They wouldn't be so happy if they walked a mile in my shoes!"

We see them as phony, Pollyanna, or just plain naïve, until we hear their story and understand the hardship they endured, which will forever be a part of their lives. Their struggles got them to a point where they can help you through your struggle.

Behind their smiles are hardships, illness, memories of lost loved ones, and even horror stories that you may never have the capacity to understand.

These are the people you will remember for a lifetime. They are the ones who will stand by you in your time of need because they have been there themselves. These are truly the most beautiful people you will ever meet.

During our lifetime, we will have the opportunity to meet a few of these beautiful people. It could be an understanding teacher at school, a friend from college, a neighbor from the old neighborhood, a co-worker from a former job, a nurse from a hospital stay. It could be the most unlikely of people. But when you meet one of these beautiful people, you will know. Be inspired by them! Treasure them!

It is said that true beauty comes from within, and that is true. As *Kübler-Ross* observed, "People are like stained glass windows. They sparkle and shine when the sun is out, but when the darkness sets in, their true beauty is revealed only if there is a light from within."[2]

Let's celebrate that light.

Reflection: *How do you define true beauty? Can you name a beautiful person in your life? Who would that be and what makes them beautiful? How does the Hollywood version of beauty fail?*

Advent or Advil

> Come to me, all you who labor and
> are burdened, and I will give you
> rest. (Matthew 11:28, NAB)

All the way to the Saturday vigil Mass, Diane and I discussed the details of preparing for Christmas. With a three-month-old and a three-year-old, the details were exhausting.

We had to make sure we had diapers, formula, shampoo, and wipes. We purchased two car seats, a high chair, and bedding that still needed setup. As Mass began, I couldn't help but think about everything that I still needed to do.

That's when my friend Deacon Roger's homily hit home!

Deacon Roger was teaching a religion class at the grade school next door to the church. He explained that the four weeks preceding Christmas was a liturgical season.

He asked the second graders, "Do you know the name for this season?" ...Silence.

"All right then, how about a clue? The season starts with the letter A." Again, silence.

Once again, he added, "The second letter is D."

This time Andrew, from the back of the classroom, threw up his hand! "I know," he exclaimed. "Advil!"

After the congregation stopped laughing, I asked myself if my season had been Advent or Advil. That day, it was Advil!

How do we keep the season more Advent and less Advil? Here are a few things we can try:

Let's block out some time each day to be quiet and enjoy the day. I like to sit in our living room and reflect on the manger scene on the coffee table.

In the anticipation of out-of-town guests, we get fixated on everything that we need to do. Let's not get hung up on the details and miss enjoying their presence. The details will all work out.

I am going to work hard at keeping the season about Advent. How about you? Are you in the middle of the Advent season or the Advil one?

Thanks, Deacon Roger, for the reminder!

Reflections: *Has your Advent season become an Advil season? What can you do to make Advent a blessed season? Do you block out some time for reflection during Advent?*

Living Kairos Moments in a Chronos World

> This is the time of fulfillment. The
> kingdom of God is at hand. Repent,
> and believe in the gospel. (Mark
> 1:15, NAB)
>
> For Christ, while we were still help-
> less, yet died at the appointed time
> for the ungodly. (Romans 5:6 NAB)

The English language is limited in its descriptions. As you may know, the Greek language has four words for love. *Agape* describes God's love for us and our love for God. *Eros* describes physical attraction. *Philia* is the love between friends. *Storge* describes a parent's affection for their children.

The same holds true for time. The ancient Greeks had two words for time: *chronos* and *kairos*. We are all familiar with *chronos* or "clock time," as we know it. It is a quantitative measure of time kept by our chronograph watches. *Kairos* is different. It is the measure of moments, especially the right moment. *Kairos* is qualitative. You can't put it on your calendar or plan for it in any way. *Kairos* moments just happen, and you know it when it does!

In all the moments of our lives, in the pause between breaths, some moments are more valuable than others.

The moment you say your wedding vows is a *kairos* moment. Witnessing the birth of your child is a *kairos* moment. Winning the championship game is too.

Kairos moments can be smaller too. For me, a walk with Diane on the beach in Naples, Florida, can be a special moment. Hearing a song on the radio that jogs a beautiful memory from a time past can be a valuable moment.

Kairos can describe right opportunity moments as well. For example, the warm feeling we get when we put aside *chronos* time and serve others. Or, when we stop everything we are doing, to console a crying child, and throw our calendar out the window in the process, we experience an opportunity moment.

Have you ever regretted a missed opportunity? I have! We do when we allow the clock to limit our "Kodak Moments."

Advent is the perfect time to focus on those special moments. Shopping for the perfect gift, decorating our homes, and planning the perfect holiday meal make it a daunting task.

This Advent season, let's try to slow down, find a quiet place, and enjoy being in the moment.

Sit in front of the beautiful Christmas tree that you worked so hard to decorate and enjoy it! Try saying the rosary in front of the manger scene in the living room. Enjoy a conversation with your grandchild on what's happening in his or her life.

What happened in a manger over 2,000 years ago is still available today. We just need to make it a priority to stay in the moment. Let's mark this Christmas in the quality of *kairos* "right moments." If not, then the birth of our Lord and Savior will simply become another past date on our calendar.

Have a blessed Advent season.

Reflections: *Have you had any* kairos *moments in your life? What do you do to stay in the moment to enjoy the little things that really matter? What is your most memorable* kairos *moment?*

Living in a Connected World

> Rejoice always. Pray without ceas-
> ing. In all circumstances give
> thanks, for this is the will of God
> for you in Christ Jesus. (1 Thessa-
> lonians 5:16–18)

We are living in a connected world. Smart phones have put instant communications in the hands of everyone. We read articles about the connected car, home, and workplace. It seems the world is a text message or tweet away.

Young people will text their friends twenty or thirty times a day. Many will take their smart phones to bed with them in case they get a late-night text.

I've even seen a businessman wearing his Bluetooth headset while swimming with his kids! We have a *need* to connect.

Wouldn't it be great if we could have the same instant communication with God? Have a moral dilemma? Send a text to God. Have a problem with your love life? God is a text message away.

Well you can! And you don't even need to spend $1,000 on the new iPhone X. It's free!

Here are a few ways to stay connected to God in the same way:

1. Include God in your daily thoughts. If we text our friends twenty to thirty times a day, why not send a mental message to God several times a day? It is what Saint Paul meant when he said we should pray without ceasing (1 Thessalonians 5:17):

    "Thank you, God, for the sunshine!"

"God, please help me get through this argument with my spouse."

"God, calm my anxiety about the presentation I am about to give at work."

It's easy! And you can do it in a few seconds.

2. Take God along when you go to bed, instead of keeping your smart phone under your pillow. Try bringing the Lord along with night prayer, a Bible reading or reflection from a good book.

3. Stay connected to God in the car. Try praying a Rosary or Chaplet of Divine Mercy on the way home from work. I find that it helps me to relax and leave the pressures of work behind and be more attentive to my wife and family.

4. Use social media to say connected. There are many great Facebook pages and groups that you can join. The Catholic Bloggers Network, Top Catholic Blogs, Inspire Me Please, True Catholicism can help you stay connected.

5. There's an app for that. Try adding some great Catholic and Christian apps to your smart phone and use them daily. Some of my favorites are, IBrevary HD, Catholic Mega, Prayer Chain and Laudate.

Living in a connected world is great, but let's not forget to stay connected to God! It's easy if you make it a priority.

Reflections: *How do you keep God in your day-to-day life? Do you have a time each day when you unplug from your smart phone and computer? Have you downloaded any apps to keep God in your day?*

Quit Your Complaining

> If you are not grateful for the
> things you have, what makes you
> think you will be grateful for the
> things you want?[3] —Tony Agnesi

Every March, Diane and I are blessed to spend the month in sunny Naples, Florida. We love the nearby Vanderbilt Beach. We walk the beach every morning for an hour and a half. We are so grateful to share this time together. Every year, I comment on how I missed my life's calling as a beach bum!

Naples is an upscale city, and most of the people there are retired, successful folks from other parts of the country and seasonal vacationers. I love everything about the area except for one thing. In the twenty-plus years we have been coming here, I continue to be amazed by the ungratefulness in the atmosphere. You would think that with the beautiful sunshine and nearly perfect sunny days, everyone would be in a grateful, cheerful mood. Unfortunately, that doesn't seem to be the case. People in Naples are always complaining about something. Somewhere along the way, being grateful for your blessings has disappeared.

> And whatever you do, in word or in
> deed, do everything in the name of
> the Lord Jesus, giving thanks to
> God the Father through him. (Colossians 3:17, NAB)

What do they complain about? Here is sample of what I overheard in just one day:

A wealthy woman complained that her smart phone battery wasn't lasting as long as it should. She blamed the sales clerk at the phone store.

A man complained, at the Ritz-Carlton, that he had to wait more than five minutes to get his drink refilled. He wanted his drink for free.

A woman at the coffee shop complained that the foam heart on her cappuccino was misshaped and wanted it replaced.

A young girl arrived at Dunkin' Donuts in her daddy's Tesla and ordered a jelly doughnut with the jelly on the side and was disturbed that they couldn't fulfill her request. She reluctantly took the regular jelly doughnut (with the jelly inside) and paid for it with Apple Pay on her iPhone 7.

An elderly woman complained that there would be a thirty-minute wait to be seated in a popular restaurant. Her husband offered, "What else do you have to wait for besides death?" I liked him.

As I walked the beach, I smiled and said good morning to everyone I passed. Of the many people I recently greeted one morning, only one responded, "Good morning." Most ignored me, turned their heads away, or even worse, looked at me in disgust.

My point is that, even in arguably the sunniest, prettiest city on the gulf coast, people can't even say good morning. And for some reason they *always* find something to complain about.

Gratitude and humility just doesn't seem to exist!

> Thanks be to God for his indescribable gift! (2 Corinthians 9:15, NAB)

I was almost ready to give up on humanity when I had an encounter with a migrant worker.

His skin was dark and stained from too much sun exposure. His hands were chapped and cut. His clothes dirty from the fields.

As we made eye contact, I smiled and said, "Hello."

"Hello," he quickly responded.

"How are you?" was my automatic response.

He paused for a moment, raised his hands toward heaven, tipped back his head and rolled his eyes skyward, and didn't say a thing; not a single word. Without speaking he spoke volumes!

Without him saying a word, I heard:

Thank you, God, for my life.

Thank you, God, for being able to support my family.

Thank you for all the blessings you have given me.

Without speaking, he restored my faith in humanity. This man understood that everything is a gift from God, and gratitude and humility lead to happiness.

Quite a contrast, right? So, I ask you, who is happier?

On one of our beach walks, Diane and I agreed that for the entire vacation we were not going to complain about anything. Every time one of us complained (OK, mostly me) she would stop me, and I would have to express gratitude. After a while it became second nature.

I can honestly say that when you are conscious of your complaining and try to stop and instead find something to be thankful for, it works! Why not give it a try?

Reflections: *Do you know someone that is always complaining? How does it make you feel? Do you ever join in on the complaining?*

Well Known or Worth Knowing

> When he arrived and saw the
> grace of God, he rejoiced and
> encouraged them all to remain
> faithful to the Lord in firmness
> of heart, for he was a good
> man, filled with the Holy Spirit
> and faith. And a large number
> of people was added to the
> Lord. (Acts 11:23–24, NAB)

We live in a time of instant stardom and notoriety. People go from relative obscurity to fame overnight. Whether it's American Idol, The Voice, Dancing with the Stars, a cable reality show, or an Instagram post that goes viral, someone is only a heartbeat away from being well-known.

It seems like this desire for celebrity status has become the pursuit of many, and being a better person has either taken a back seat or isn't even part of the equation. Being well-known has replaced being a person worth knowing.

Is that really what we should want? Is that going to make us a better person, the person God meant us to be?

What many people discover is that popularity is fleeting. You can be on top of the world today and completely rejected tomorrow. Popularity is not relevant to God's plan.

Just as being well-known is fleeting, being worth knowing is timeless. Living a virtuous life of kindness, honesty, compassion, forgiveness, and gratitude has a lasting value that attracts people, not because of celebrity, but because they sense you are worth knowing.

So, what does the Bible have to say about being worth knowing? How can we spend our time being a person worth knowing? In the book of Acts, we read that we must be faithful to the Lord and be filled with the Holy Spirit and faith.

> He said to him, "You shall love the Lord, your God, with all your heart, with all your soul, and with all your mind." (Matthew 22:37, NAB)

1. **Love God.** If we love God and follow Him, we lay the groundwork for being a person worth knowing. We realize that everything we have is a gift from God and we should love Him, as we learn in Matthew.

2. **Love Others.** If we are God's people then we will be known by the compassion for the less fortunate, kindness to others, our humble attitude, gentleness, and patience with those who are struggling with life's challenges.

> Put on then, as God's chosen ones, holy and beloved, heartfelt compassion, kindness, humility, gentleness, and patience. (Colossians 3:12, NAB)

3. **We Must Walk by Faith**. As we learn in 2 Corinthians, we walk by faith, not by sight. Our righteousness comes from our faith that God has things under control. When we are out of options and have tried to go it alone, we realize that when we turn our lives over to Him, we begin to walk by faith knowing that God is with us.

Remember, popularity is fleeting, and righteousness is timeless. Let's spend our energy on becoming a better person; a person worth knowing.

> For in it is revealed the righteousness of God from faith to faith; as

it is written, "The one who is righteous by faith will live." (Romans
1:17, NAB)

I remember an anonymous quote about the definition of hell. It
goes, "On your last day on earth, the person you became will meet
the person you could have become. Let's try to work at becoming
that person, the one God meant for us to be!

*Reflections: What is the difference between well-known and worth know-
ing? Which do you strive for? Why do you think popularity has become the
goal rather than aiming towards becoming a better person?*

A Leap of Faith

When the disciples saw him walking
on the sea they were terrified. "It is
a ghost," they said, and they cried
out in fear. At once [Jesus] spoke to
them, "Take courage, it is I; do not
be afraid." Peter said to him in reply, "Lord, if it is you, command
me to come to you on the water."
He said, "Come." Peter got out of
the boat and began to walk on the
water toward Jesus. But when he
saw how [strong] the wind was he
became frightened; and, beginning
to sink, he cried out, "Lord, save
me!" Immediately Jesus stretched
out his hand and caught him, and
said to him, "O you of little faith,
why did you doubt?" (Matthew
14:26–31, NAB)

There is a popular story by Danish Philosopher, Soren Kierke-gaard, of a man trapped on the edge of a cliff:

> There was a roaring fire just a few yards away that would certainly reach him in minutes and he would be consumed by the flames.
>
> As he looked over the edge, a voice called out to him, "Jump!" He glanced down and saw nothing but smoke and darkness and replied, "But I can't see you!"
>
> The voice from the bottom of the cliff re-sponded, "Jump, anyway. I can see *you*."[4]

Do you hear our Lord calling you? What is Jesus calling you to do that has you on the edge of a personal cliff? Do you believe strongly enough to take a leap of faith? Do you trust that the Lord will be there to catch you with outstretched arms?

We all face these personal cliffs in our lifetime. Marriage, a new job, moving to a different town, going back to college, having that dangerous surgery, or starting a new business or ministry, are all situations that cause us to stop, look over that personal cliff, knowing that a lack of action will cause us to be consumed in the fire of indifference.

> Faith is the realization of what is hoped for and evidence of things not seen. (Hebrews 11:1, NAB)

Many times, the fear of the unknown paralyzes us, yet not deciding *is* making a decision not to take the leap. Remember, you have to leap to begin!

To have faith is to jump even when we cannot see what awaits us. It's scary. The fear of the unknown always is scary. But if we be-lieve that Jesus waits with outstretched arms to catch us, to protect us, and to save us, it becomes a little less scary.

Do you hear God calling you to take a leap of faith? Do you believe enough to jump?

A sad summary of life could be described as could have, would have, and should have. Come on, take the leap of faith!

Reflections: *What is keeping you from taking a leap of faith? Does the fear of being laughed at by society stop you? Do you hear God calling you to take the leap?*

Love and Truth Shall Meet

> "Love and truth will meet; justice
> and peace will kiss. Truth will spring
> from the earth; justice will look
> down from heaven." (Psalm 85:11-
> 12 NAB)

A wise rabbi once said that the world is sustained by three things: justice, truth, and peace. When justice is done, truth is served, and peace is achieved.

In Catholic social teaching, we understand that nonviolence denotes peace with justice; that we should be peaceful, truthful, and loving in our relationships, especially with those who don't share our opinions.

Dr. Martin Luther King Jr. embraced these nonviolent tenants as well. He understood that peace cannot be achieved by conflict, rioting, and unrest. It can only be achieved by a constant call for justice, stating the truth, and softening the hearts with love. When we approach social justice with love and truth, justice and peace will follow.

Mahatma Gandhi said, "Nonviolence is not a garment to be put on and off at will. Its seat is in the heart, and it must be an inseparable part of our being."[5]

Sadly, that's not what we see on the evening news today. In our country, we see rioting, looting, and violence. We see young men losing their lives due to excessive reactions; policemen killed while sitting in their patrol cars, and people overreacting with so-called leaders fueling the fire of violence.

Across the world we see beheading, young school girls kidnapped, and men and women martyred for their faith.

The wise rabbi would teach that this is not the way to peace. Catholic social teaching would argue that we should peacefully get people together to find a solution. One of the greatest leaders of social justice in the 20th century, Martin Luther King, would beg us to stop the violence, and Gandhi would tell us that "An eye for an eye will only make the whole world blind."[6] What has happened since the death of Doctor King to undo all of his work? Where are the leaders, especially religious leaders, who will continue the legacy of nonviolent protesting?

Our country needs leadership, not neat thirty-second sound bites on the news. We need people who understand the process to initiate the conversation, do the hard work, usually behind the scenes, and move our country to a better understanding of the truth.

The world needs leadership, not the savagery that is disguised as faith.

What we don't need are leaders, with their own political agendas, lining their pockets while their followers riot in the streets, where much of the world is unsafe.

Where is the next Gandhi, Mandela, Kennedy, or King? Where are the leaders that can show us a better way? Most of the world's religions teach these same principles of love and truth, justice and peace. We need leadership that can get this done. I hope and pray that these leaders will emerge.

Until then, I'll keep praying for peace.

Reflections: *What are you doing to support peace? Where do we find the leaders to show us the way to peace? What are you doing to promote social justice?*

Who Do You Say That I AM?

> When Jesus went into the region of Caesarea Philippi he asked his disciples, "Who do people say that the Son of Man is?" They replied, "Some say John the Baptist, others Elijah, still others Jeremiah or one of the prophets." He said to them, "But who do you say that I am?" Simon Peter said in reply, "You are the Messiah, the Son of the living God." (Matthew 16:13–16, NAB)

In Matthew's Gospel, Jesus asks his disciples *two* questions: Who do the people say that I am? Who do *you* say that I am?

What strikes me as important in Jesus's question is that it seems that people are more concerned with following the crowd, than following Jesus.

Recently, it seems that the label of Democrat or Republican, liberal or conservative, straight or gay, is paramount to how most people form their opinions. These labels seem to trump the teachings of our Christian faith. If we are truly Christians, and we have the Bible and the Magisterium as our guides, then many of these issues should be clear to us.

> Right is right even if no one is doing it, wrong is wrong, even if everyone is doing it.[7] —Saint Augustine of Hippo

But are they?

I am sure that your mother or grandmother has said to you more than once, "If all your friends were jumping off a cliff, would you jump too?" Usually, this response comes after you have whined, "But *all* my friends are doing it!"

You see, when it comes to faith and morals, we can't just go along with prevailing public opinion. Wrong is always wrong, even if everyone agrees to the contrary!

Let's put all man-made labels aside. I am a Christian first, before I am a liberal or conservative, Democrat or Republican. I have a guide, Jesus, who leads me on the right path.

The modern world says many things about Jesus. He was a good guy, a prophet, a man ahead of his times. He is right up there with Moses, Mohammed, and Buddha. You've heard them all. They say nothing about Jesus as God, Our Lord, and Savior.

But who do you say Jesus is? If he is your Savior, your Lord and God, then, don't you think His teachings should trump the lemmings leading us to this culture of death?

Let's make it a point to be Christians. Let's see what the Bible has to say about issues, so that it can help us form a true Christian conscience. Then we will understand the question, "Who do you say that I am?"

Reflection: *Who is Jesus to you? Who do your friends say that Jesus is to them? Are you a Christian first, before Liberal or Conservative?*

Green with Envy

> Rejoice with those who rejoice,
> weep with those who weep. (Romans 12:15, NAB)

Have you ever reacted to someone's good fortune with envy? It's scary. We surprise ourselves because we should be happy for them and rejoice in their good fortune. Nevertheless, something within us resents it.

It is one of the seven deadly sins, and all of us, Christian and non-Christian, can get caught up in its debilitating web.

In our narcissistic, self-centered, me-oriented society, we all become consumer coveters. We are sold by advertising that we deserve all sorts of things that we can't afford or aren't willing to work hard enough to achieve. We have to "keep up with the Kardashians!"

Every young girl wants the wedding that costs her family six figures and can't understand why Mom and Dad balk at the cost. After all, the media says she deserves her "special day!"

Every couple covets the huge house, swimming pool, a garage full of expensive luxury cars, and a wardrobe right off the Paris runway. When we can't have them, we are envious of those who do.

Worse yet, we elevate those people who do achieve celebrity status. Our envy makes them stars!

Let's not confuse envy with jealousy. Jealousy is a fear of losing what we have to another. Envy is rejoicing in someone's suffering and weeping at their blessings! We are fixated on counting other people's blessings, while ignoring our own.

What is the correct Christian response to our feelings of envy?

Saint Paul, in Romans 12:9–21, warned that envy was a danger, even in the early Christian communities. He instructed us in mutual or, as we call it, brotherly love. Whether it's a promotion, engagement, or a new grandchild, we are called to rejoice with those who rejoice. If it is an illness, disease, or death, we are called to weep with those who weep.

Let's spend some time each week being grateful for what we have, the gifts and skills we possess, and the blessings we have received. Let's pray that we can have a healthy belief in ourselves and banish envy from our hearts.

If envy undermines happiness, then gratitude and mutual love for one anther will help us put the sin of envy behind us, to lead a happier, more grateful life.

Reflection: *What is the correct Christian response to our feelings of envy? Do you ever find yourself envious of others? Do you agree that envy undermines happiness?*

Be Passionate

> He said to him, "You shall love the
> Lord, your God, with all your heart,
> with all your soul, and with all your
> mind. This is the greatest and the
> first commandment. The second is
> like it: You shall love your neighbor
> as yourself." (Matthew 22:37–39,
> NAB)

I am a passionate person. I live life passionately. I am passionate about my marriage, my family, my friends, my work, my writing and speaking, fishing, golfing, and most importantly, I am passionate about my Catholic faith.

When Jesus said that we should love God with all of our heart, soul, and mind, He meant that we should love God passionately! And your neighbor? Love them passionately!

Too many people lead lukewarm lives. They enjoy many things, but aren't passionate about anything; not their families, not their job, not their interests. Nothing sets them on fire with passion.

There is an old saying that if you love anything at a moderate level, it's a hobby. But if you are "On Fire" and are willing to give it all you've got, it's a passion.

In my years as a businessman, I've been asked what my number one quality is that I look for in a new employee.

That's easy: passion! More than experience, credentials, degrees, or special training, I'd say passion! Give me a passionate person and I'll teach them the rest.

People love passionate people! They are contagious, engaging, motivational, and inspiring. They are on fire with what they do. They willingly share it, express it, and learn more about it and continually "stoke the fire" with new energy.

The same is true for faith. Jesus is not asking us to be lukewarm about our faith. We should be on fire! We should be passionate about it, share it with others, and be willing to learn more about it, so that we can defend it.

If you are passionate about learning to play the guitar, you don't do it one hour a week, on Sunday mornings. You play constantly, until your fingers bleed and calluses form. Hour after hour, day after day, you play the guitar, constantly improving, until your passion and joy entertains and motivates others.

So, what makes us think we can love God one hour a week, on Sunday morning? We need to attend Mass, read the Bible, study the saints, and spend time with people passionate about their faith. We can join prayer groups, Bible studies, and apostolates that are natural extensions of those other things in life that we are passionate about. There are many organizations that could use your expertise.

Don't be afraid to show your passion. Bring passion to everything you do. Remember, people love passionate people.

Want to be happy? Be passionate about something and see how much happier you become. Then, extend that passion to your faith and watch your happiness turn to joy.

Reflections: *What are you passionate about? Are you passionate about your faith? What drives your passions?*

Be Not Afraid

> The LORD is my light and my sal-
> vation; whom should I fear? The
> LORD is my life's refuge; of whom
> am I afraid? (Psalm 27:1, NAB)

> The LORD is with me; I am not
> afraid; what can mortals do against
> me? (Psalm 118:6, NAB)

I read a while back that the Bible has 365 uses of the phrase "fear not" or "be not afraid." I haven't been able to verify that, but I can tell you that it is one of the most used themes in the Bible.

Fear is the one emotion that keeps us from trying new things, achieving our goals, and taking the first step. Maintaining status quo is comfortable. We fear change. When fearful, we don't have to think or plan, and we become paralyzed. Our inactions breed fear and doubt.

There's an old adage that the only people that like change are wet babies! It's true. Most people would rather stay right where they are, in a comfortable rut, fearful they might make a mistake.

We want to return to college, but we fear it will take too long to finish.

We want to get a new job, but just can't get around to updating that resume.

We want to meet new people, find friends, and maybe even some-one that we can spend the rest of our lives with, but we are too afraid to sign up on a dating site.

The same holds true with our faith. We want to be better Chris-tians, better Catholics. We want to do more, pray more, get involved in activities and ministries, but we fear taking the first step.

The problem with that thinking is that time will pass either way. You might as well get started.

The hardest thing to do is to take the first step. But what are we afraid of? We have God's word that he is with us, our refuge, our strength and salvation. Shouldn't that be a good enough reason to start?

Here are a few things we can do to get the ball rolling:

1. **Take baby steps.** Sit down and write down the things you want to do. Then break it down into small steps and take the first one right away.

Do you want to improve your prayer life? Add a morning offering, or an extra Hail Mary, or recite the chaplet while you drive to work.

Do you want to get a new job? Spend thirty minutes updating your resume—today!

2. **Move in the direction of your goals.** As you begin, make sure that you are always moving in a positive direction. Try not to get into the "two steps forward, one step back" trap. When you complete one baby step, immediately move on to the next.
3. **Ask yourself, "What have I got to lose?"** Remember, time will pass whether you take action or not. What will it cost you if you do nothing?

Come on, you can do it! You've got God on your side. Get up and get going, right now.

Reflection: Do you feel your inaction is keeping you from achieving your goals? Do you feel you are moving in the direction of your goals? What about the idea of baby steps? What might you gain by taking action?

That Your Joy May Be Complete

"As the Father loves me, so I also
love you. Remain in my love. If you
keep my commandments, you will
remain in my love, just as I have
kept my Father's commandments
and remain in his love. I have told
you this so that my joy may be in
you and your joy may be complete.
(John 15:9–11, NAB)

Joy, the second fruit of the spirit from Galatians 5:22, is a word
used over 100 times in the Old and New Testaments, but what is
it? What is joy?

Ask most people and they will say that it is happiness, but a true
Christian understanding of joy goes beyond happiness. It's deeper.
It's from within, and it isn't dependent on circumstances or good
fortune. It's not a fleeting feeling that is here when good things
happen and gone when we are in distress.

Joy, true joy, is a gift. It is a gift from God to those who belong to
him.

It is an abiding sense that God is in control, and no matter what
happens, we have His promise of salvation and eternal life. Have
you ever noticed that as your relationship with Jesus deepens, so
does your joy? God wants us to be joyful, and His joy is there for
the taking.

It is a gift that grows out of faith, gratitude, grace and love, the
delight in being alive.

He not only wants us to be joyful, but to delight in the joy of others as well.

> May the God of hope fill you with
> all joy and peace in believing, so
> that you may abound in hope by
> the power of the holy Spirit. (Romans 15:13, NAB)

There is an old adage that the Dominican sisters would share with me. They would spell the word, J-O-Y and then would offer themselves to J-Jesus, O-Others, Y-Yourself, in that order! If you want to be joyful, put Jesus first, others second, and yourself last.

As an adult, I have learned that this is the formula for servant leadership. Bringing joy to others fuels our joy as well. As we serve others, God will always keep our joy "tank" on full! It is His gift to us.

Want joy? Ask for it! Pray for it! Strengthen your relationship with Jesus, read scripture, and serve others!

The second fruit of the Holy Spirit is JOY, so that Jesus's joy may be in you and your joy may be complete.

Be joyful, my friend; it is a gift from God for each of us.

Reflections: *What makes happiness different than joy? Have you ever felt true joy? What was the occasion and how did it make you feel? What can we do to have more joy in our lives?*

Embrace the Ordinary

> For most of life, nothing wonderful
> happens. If you don't enjoy getting
> up and working and finishing your
> work and sitting down to a meal
> with family or friends, then the
> chances are you're not going to be
> very happy. If someone bases his
> [or her] happiness on major events
> like a great job, huge amounts of
> money, a flawlessly happy marriage
> or a trip to Paris, that person isn't
> going to be happy much of the
> time. If, on the other hand, happi-
> ness depends on a good breakfast,
> flowers in the yard, a drink or a
> nap, then we are more likely to live
> with quite a bit of happiness.[8] —
> Andy Rooney

Most people spend their lives in pursuit of the extraordinary. We look at the lives of celebrities, glorify their excesses, and wish that our lives could be more like theirs.

It causes young women to desire the same wedding as a Holly-wood movie star; spending money her parents don't have on her extraordinary day. It causes the young man to buy the BMW, when a Kia is all he can afford.

We have a fear of being ordinary. We are ashamed if we don't have the same or better status than others.

We fear that our lives don't matter, that our work isn't recognized, that we are simply ordinary, not special.

Think of all the special, extraordinary moments you can recall in your life. If you added them all together, they might make up one percent of your time on earth.

Were those moments exciting? Yes. Important? Sure. But what about the other 99 percent of your life? What about all those other days, the ordinary ones? Not the birthdays, anniversaries, vacations, parties, or winning the big game, but what about the quiet ordinary days?

We need to embrace those too!

If we are so consumed with the big event this weekend, then we miss so much.

We miss the beauty of the day.

We miss the changing of the seasons.

We miss our baby's smile.

We miss the way blueberries turn milk purple in the bottom of your cereal bowl.

We miss the daffodils and tulips that welcome spring, and the sound of water splashing in the pool as kids giggle with summer delight.

We miss sitting by a fire on a chilly autumn night, sharing stories with friends over a cold beer.

When we look at the extraordinary life of Jesus, it was for the most part pretty ordinary. Nothing special about being born in a manger, traveling on foot, spending his first thirty years as a carpenter working with his dad, avoiding celebrity status by asking people not to tell of the miracles he performed. Nevertheless, his rising from the dead was the most extraordinary event in history!

Instead of fearing being ordinary, Jesus simply embraced it.

Furthermore, He accepts us just as we are, with our fears, failures, and shortcomings. He accepts us, sinners that we all are, with open arms and eternal salvation. He accepts us as ordinary people capable of extraordinary things.

Frequently, we hear stories of heroism. We hear of a soldier jumping on a grenade to save his platoon, or the fireman who goes back into a house engulfed in flames to save a young child. We hear of people who use their vacation time to help a town rebuild after being damaged by a tornado.

Most of these heroes would call themselves ordinary. The difference is that at some moment they rose to the occasion to do something special, something extraordinary.

We hear it said that we should live in the moment, not relive the past, or spend time worrying about tomorrow. We need to drink in everything around us, the ordinary things, and when the extraordinary happens, we can enjoy it more fully.

Let's thank God for every moment, even the ordinary ones.

Reflection: Do you find yourself missing the ordinary in search of the extraordinary? What can we do to embrace the ordinary occurrences in life? Are you comfortable with your ordinary life?

It Only Takes One

Do not fear: I am with you; be not dismayed: I am your God. I will strengthen you, and help you, and uphold you with my right hand of justice. (Isaiah 41:10, NAB)

I have always been impressed with the power in the number one. It only takes one person, one kind word, one thought, or one good deed to change the world.

One is a very powerful number.

Remember that one teacher that stands out beyond all others. The one who believed in you, took a special interest in you, and helped you gain the confidence to succeed.

Remember that one coach that pushed you harder than anyone else on the team. Remember the day when you realized that he did so because he thought you were special and had the potential to be a college or professional athlete.

Remember that one friend who stuck by you all these years, through college, marriages, families, moves to other states, good and bad times, always being the one you could really count on.

Remember the one employer, or older associate, who shared her knowledge and experience with you, who you now credit with guiding and mentoring your career.

Yes, one is a powerful number!

Do you know that you can be that one person for someone? You never forget the person that was there for you when no one else stepped up. You can be the one person they will always remember.

It only takes one negative comment to kill a dream, but one encouraging word can set a person on a course of success and the fulfillment of lifelong dreams. One moment can change everything!

For me, these people and their kindnesses are etched in my mind. I can remember the moments as if it were yesterday. I recall the exact words that were shared, the encouragement, the special feeling of the moment.

I bet that you can remember the people and moments that changed your life, as well.

There are some people who never hear words of encouragement, never have someone who will believe in them, stick with them, mentor them, and love them. They live their lives under a constant barrage of negativism.

There is an old saying it takes one tree to make a thousand matches, but it only takes one match to burn a thousand trees. That's what happens when you spew the venom of your negative comments on your spouse, your children, your friends, coworkers, and fellow students.

Let's remember that there is power in your words. Negative words can kill a dream, but positive words can start the journey to a dream come true.

What about your faith journey? It only takes one faith, one savior, one baptism, to change our lives forever. To be born again by water and spirit, to be sons and daughters of the one true God. We will never forget the people, especially the one person that brought us to a better understanding of our faith and helped us to find forgiveness, redemption, and salvation.

Yes, God is the One that can change our lives forever. He is the same yesterday, today, and forever. If we follow Him, put our faith in Him, He promises to be that friend that is always there for us.

You never forget the ones that helped you on your journey, and you'll never forget the ones who brought you to the Lord.

Let's all strive to be that one person that will make a difference in the life of a friend or stranger.

Reflections: *Have you ever been that one person for another? Can you remember the one teacher, coach, or friend that helped you become the person you are today? Have you ever mentored a friend?*

A Final Thought

We have come to the end of my stories. I hope that one or more have become a blessing to you. I pray that the book has, in some way, motivated you to take action and support those who are going through difficulties.

I hope you decided to put feet under your faith and turn your misery into a ministry. I can promise you that despite all the suffering and pain, you will be living a joyful life that only comes from service to others.

That, my friend, is one of the secrets of finding joy. May God bless you with a joy-filled life of love and service!

Reference List

Chapter One—God's Grace in Service

[1] Anthony DeStefano, *Ten Prayers God Always Says Yes To* (New York: Image Books-Doubleday, 2009), p. 26.

[2] Bruce Wilkinson, *You Were Born for This* (Colorado Springs: Multnomah Books, 2009)

[3] Anthony DeStefano, *Ten Prayers God Always Says Yes To* (New York: Image Books-Doubleday, 2009), p. 26.

[4] Teresa of Calcutta, Jaya Chaliha and Edward Le Joly, *The Joy in Loving, a Guide to Daily Living,* (New York: Penguin Books; Reprint edition, 2000), p.126.

[5] Mahatma Gandhi, "Address to the U.S. Congress" (Washington DC: Congressional Record, House, Vol. 153, pt. 119, October 2, 2007).

[6] Gary Morsh and Dean Nelson, *The Power of Serving Others,* (Oklahoma City: Dust Jacket Press, 2006), p.2.

Chapter Two—God's Grace in Taking Action

[1] Tony Agnesi, *Girls with Purple Hair,* last modified August 31, 2014. https://tonyagnesi.com/2014/08/girls-with-purple-hair/

Chapter Three—God's Grace in Hard Times

[1] Teresa of Calcutta, Jaya Chaliha and Edward Le Joly, *The Joy in Loving, a Guide to Daily Living,* (Sydney: Penguin Books; Reprint edition, 2000), p. 121.

[2] *Ibid,* p.232

[3] Rafael Merry del Val, "Litany of Humility." ewtn.com. n.d. https://www.ewtn.com/devotionals/prayers/humility.htm

[4][Pope] Francis, "National Catholic Reporter," https://www.ncronline.org/blogs/francis-chronicles/francis-whoever-judges-and-scorns-others-corrupt-and-hypocrite

[5]Thomas of Selano, "The Life of Saint Francis: Remembrance of the Desire of a Soul." Franciscan Intellectual Tradition. *FA:ED,* vol. 1, 171. n.d. https://franciscantradition.org/francis-of-assisi-early-documents/the-saint/the-life-of-saint-francis-by-thomas-of-celano/612-fa-ed-1-page-171

[6] Cheryl Rainfield, *Scars,* (Lodi: WestSide Books, 2012), p. 43.

[7] Kahlil Gibran, *Spiritual Sayings of Kahlil Gibran,* (New York): Citadel Press, 1962), p. 87.

[8] Sheen, Fulton J., "Daily Catholic Quote – from Venerable Fulton J. Sheen," Integrated Catholic Life. 12 Nov. 2016. http://www.integratedcatholiclife.org/2016/11/daily-catholic-quote-from-venerable-fulton-j-sheen-44/

Chapter Four—God's Grace in the Virtues

[1] Elizabeth Kübler-Ross, *On Death and Dying,* (New York: Scribner; Reprint edition, 2011), p. 114.

[2] *ibid,* p.145.

[3] Tony Agnesi, "Gratitude," Finding God's Grace, 2017, (https://tonyagnesi.com/2017/03/gratitude/)

[4] Soren Kierkegaard, *The Concept of Anxiety*, (Copenhagen: Liveright, 2015), p, 181.

[5] Mahatma Gandhi, "Address to the U.S. Congress" (Washington DC: Congressional Record, House, Vol. 153, pt. 119, October 2, 2007).

[6] *Ibid.*

[7] Augustine of Hippo, *Confessions Oxford World Classics* , (London: Oxford University Press; 2009), p.284.

[8] Andy Rooney, *My War*, (New York:Publicaffairs; Public affairs ed. Edition, 2008), p. 114.

Acknowledgements

There are so many people to thank for their help in both the writing and publishing of *A Storyteller's Guide to Joyful Service*.

Thank you to my editor, Michelle Buckman, for her late nights editing the book, to Virginia Lieto for proofreading, and, to Barbara Gaskell and Jeff Flaherty, for the rough edit.

Thank you to my wife Diane for her weekly spelling and grammar checks.

A special thanks to Chuck Collins for his continuous encouragement early on in my writing, until he passed away.

Thank you to the staff of Living Bread Radio in Canton, Ohio, especially Barb Gaskell, Molly Romano, Daniel Clark, Michael Roberts, Suzanne Houseman, Betty DeMarco, Sharon Shriver, T.O. Bennett and the members of their board.

Thank you to the staff and board of the Community Pregnancy Center, and the Embrace Clinic and Care Center, especially Rhonda Didado, Diane O'Neill, and Pat Shea.

Thank you to the staff of the Medina County Jail, especially chaplains Larry and Susan Jarvis, Sgt. Tammy Singletary, Sheriff Tom Miller and Sheriff Neil Hassinger.

Thank you to the Diocese of Cleveland Ministry to the Incarcerated, especially Sister Rita Mary Harwood, and to our ministry team, led by Connie Ebaugh, and to Deacon Roger Klaas, George

Fink, Cathy Anderson, Darryl McQuate, Theresa Virkler, and Sister Joan Rader.

Thank you to the organizations ministering to the homeless including Haven of Rest, Springtime of Hope, St Bernard's, Project Homeless Connect and many others.

Thank you to the Catholic blogging community and the Catholic Writers Guild especially Virginia Lieto, Michael Seagriff, Elizabeth Reardon, Nancy Ward, Jeannie Ewing, Kerri Lynn Bishop, Brian Gill, Blanca Hernandez, and Allison Gingras.

Thank you to Shalom Tidings Magazine, especially Mary Job, for including my stories in their wonderful publication.

Made in the USA
San Bernardino, CA
11 January 2020

62657922R00098